Never
Say
Die

getting deep in the book of Revelation

Steve Keels and Lawrence Kimbrough

NEVER SAY DIE
Getting Deep in the Book of Revelation
Copyright © 2004 by Broadman & Holman Publishers

Broadman & Holman Publishers
Nashville, Tennessee
broadmanholman.com

ISBN 0-8054-2854-2

Dewey Decimal Classification: 226.4
Subject Heading: Bible. N.T. Revelation—Commentaries

Printed in the United States of America
2 3 4 5 07 06 05 04
EB

What's Going On?

Maybe one of the best ways to introduce Revelation is with a true story.

Karen Watson didn't grow up wanting to be a missionary. But when she gave her heart to Christ as a young woman, she threw herself into her faith with everything she had. After several years of mentoring college-age women and taking a handful of short-term mission trips, she sold her house and car and committed to full-time foreign duty.

Her first assignment was a dangerous one—assisting with refugee and relief work in Jordan and northern Iraq. It was so dangerous, in fact, that upon her arrival, she felt the need to write out a special note, seal it in an envelope, and keep it with her belongings—to be opened and read only in the event of her death.

On March 14, 2004, she and four other missionaries spent the day scouting locations for a water purification project. Late in the afternoon, while heading back to their quarters for supper, their pickup was ambushed by armed Iraqis. Everyone in her group was shot. Only one survived. Karen was killed instantly.

During a memorial service soon after the tragedy, the pastor of her California church read from the sealed letter Karen had written. It summed up her reason for living, her perspective on what serving Christ is all about. It read, "To obey is my objective. To suffer is expected. His glory will be my reward."[1]

You may think Revelation is mostly about figuring out when Jesus is coming back, who the antichrist is, and how the end-times puzzle fits together. More than anything, though, Revelation is a book that talks about the things Karen Watson knew and experienced—obedience, suffering, and ultimate victory. It's not just about how these things applied in Bible times, or even how they apply on a Middle Eastern mission field, but right where you live . . . right now.

It's not merely about the last days, but about this very day.

Revelation is for you . . . and for now.

Ready to go?

This book is a commentary—a verse-by-verse explanation of what Revelation says and what it means. But it's much more than that. It's a way not only to try to understand Revelation's unusual brand of prophecy, but also to let God bring its message into your everyday life.

Revelation is more than angels and monsters. It's more than charts and graphs and curious timetables. It's a book about real life. It's a book about hope. And it's a book we're "blessed" for reading if we respond to it in obedience (1:3).

[1] Edward E. Plowman, "His Glory Will Be My Reward," *World*, Vol. 19, No. 12 (March 27, 2004), 21.

Real quick, let us give you a few tips and pointers on what to expect and how to make the most of this trip.

1] Pack your Bible.

This book won't do you much good unless your Bible's right next to it. We're not going to spoon-feed you by writing out all the verses, because you can read them for yourself. Instead, we're going to be commenting on them, helping you think about them and sort things out. So you'll need to know what the Bible says to make any sense of what we say.

2] Read ahead.

You don't have to, but it wouldn't be the worst thing in the world if you'd go ahead and read the whole book of Revelation first. It'll probably take you just over an hour to get through it, but it'll be well worth every minute. Reading a Bible book straight through really helps you understand it better. But whatever you do, be sure to read the Bible passage that goes with each section before you read our commentary notes on it.

3] Look back.

One of the most important things to know about the Bible is that it proves itself true. Only God could take dozens of writers, space them over thousands of years, and unite all their writings into one book that is totally consistent the whole way through. It's very important, then, to see what God was doing in all the different books of the Bible. This is especially true in Revelation, which fulfills and completes so many prophecies from the Old Testament. So when you come to a place that asks you to look up a verse somewhere, be sure to do it. You'll get a lot more out of the trip that way.

4] Be on the lookout.

We've added several sidebars and other features to keep you from missing anything along the way. Here's what they'll look like, and here's what they'll do for you:

D-FENCE. This will highlight key verses or topics that are foundational to Christian living and thinking. They'll help you be able to defend your faith better, to understand what others believe, and to make sharing Christ a more confident, productive experience.

DEFINITIONS. A lot of words used in the Bible—and the doctrinal terms that come from them—aren't all that easy to understand. Check here to get your fuzzy areas cleared up.

BIBLE REFERENCE. As often as possible, we'll dispatch you to another biblical location so you can see when an idea first shows up in the Scripture, or says something a different way, or gives you a better whole-Bible understanding. (Oh, and also, whenever you see a reference that just lists chapter and verse, like this—12:34, with no Bible book name—that means it's another passage from Revelation.)

HISTORY. Part of what makes the Bible hard to interpret is that we don't always know the historical settings in which it was written. These little side-notes will give you an idea of things the original Bible audience understood as common knowledge—the same way we understand things in our current culture.

TENSION. Some Bible verses—even after you've read them, and reread them, and read them some more—still don't seem to make any sense. Look for this in-text marker fairly often, where we'll do our best to help you wrestle with—and hopefully start to untangle—the toughest, knottiest passages. Sometimes we'll just have to leave it with a "we don't know for sure," but that's okay. If God's ways were always easy to understand, He wouldn't be much of a God, would He?

TRUTHQUEST QUESTIONS. We've also sprinkled in some room for you to write, to deal with some of the day-to-day implications of what you're reading in Revelation. Be sure not to skip over these or to settle for simple answers. These are important. The Bible is a living book.

5] Use this book as a devotional guide. You can
do this fairly easily by going one-by-one to the TruthQuest questions, using the passage where the question is found as your daily Bible reading, then praying or journaling your way through the answers. If nothing else, it'll give you something new to try—different from the usual devotional book or magazine—and it'll hold you for a month or so until God leads you to something else.

Who? What? Where?

Revelation's Facts

- 222 chapters
- 405 verses
- around 11,600 words
- written by the Apostle John about A.D. 95
- composed for the "seven churches" of Asia
- contains references to 32 Old Testament books
- the only book of prophecy in the New Testament

John's Bio

The writer of Revelation simply identified himself as "John" (1:4), which doesn't necessarily mean he was the same John who was in Christ's inner circle of apostles. But just about everyone feels sure that this John was the second half of the "James and John" brother duo, one of the "sons of thunder," the author of the Gospel of John and the three New Testament letters of John (First, Second, and Third).

He was a fisherman born into a fisherman family, the son of a man named Zebedee (ZEB-uh-dee). In fact, it was while he and James were "in a boat" mending nets with their dad that Jesus called these two brothers to come follow Him (Matthew 4:21-22). John, of course, appeared repeatedly in the Gospels, and again in the book of Acts, as one of the key leaders of the early church. He then revealed his tender, compassionate, yet sold-out heart for Christ in the three letters that bear his name.

According to tradition, John lived to an old age in Ephesus, one of the largest cities in the ancient world, preaching Christ and fighting false teaching until the age of 100, but not before suffering a stint in exile on an island called Patmos. This book—the "revelation of Jesus Christ"—was delivered to him sometime while he was there.

John's Book

There's no other Bible book quite like Revelation. It was a letter sent to churches in various cities, intended to be read and passed along to the next one. But instead of being a custom collection of Christian teaching (like Paul's letters were), it's filled with fantastic prophetic images and astounding symbolism—all true, but spine-tingling nonetheless.

Revelation is what Bible experts call *apocalyptic literature* (uh-POCK-uh-LIP-tic)—meaning it uses symbolic language to foretell some kind of divine intervention in the future. The book is really a fitting conclusion to the Bible, because it completes themes that were introduced as far back as Genesis and Exodus. For example, it shows how:

- the kingdom of God is finally and completely established
- sinful rebellion is punished
- humanity is restored to perfect fellowship with God

The word *revelation* simply means something that is "revealed." Biblical truth, you see, isn't actually something you dig out or discover. You don't pry it open the way you'd tug on a stuck locker or twist the top off a new jelly jar. Spiritual knowledge is revealed; God gives it to us by "revelation." In this Bible book, Jesus is both the Revealer and the One the revelation is about.

John's Reasons

Like all Scripture, Revelation was inspired by the Holy Spirit. It wasn't just a clever idea John thought up as a way of encouraging the first-century Christians. But certainly this book—written at the end of the first century, when believers were being persecuted and often killed for believing in Christ—was designed to remind God's people of the hope waiting for them in heaven. It was a call for them to endure hardship, knowing that their rest and reward would more than make up for their season of suffering.

Revelation's Interpretation

Because this book is so unique in biblical literature, it has been interpreted many different ways down through the centuries. Here are a few of the broad philosophies people have used in trying to tackle this unusual but significant slice of Scripture. These options are not totally distinct from each other. Some people borrow from more than one in figuring out what goes where:

• *Poetic-symbolic view.* Some folks think of Revelation as an epic, dramatic poem that expresses the triumph of God. They think it's sort of like an abstract painting, not intended to be taken literally, but merely an artistic device used to communicate a theme.

• *Historical-critical view.* This approach doesn't see Revelation as future-tense prophecy at all. Instead, the events of the book are all references to the historical context in which it was written: the first-century Roman Empire and the fall of Jerusalem in A.D. 70.

• *Historicist view.* Like the above view, this method (pronounced "his-TORE-uh-sist") considers most—if not all—biblical prophecy to be already fulfilled. It differs, however, by seeing Revelation as specific developments in *church history*, not just the first century.

• *Futurist view.* This says that the main thrust of Revelation concerns the future. This is also known as the *eschatological view* (ESS-kah-tuh-LODGE-ical), a variation of the word *eschatology* (ESS-kah-TAHL-ogy), meaning a study of the last things in world history.

This TruthQuest commentary will primarily take a *futurist approach*, while using insights from the other points of view where appropriate.

Revelation's Definitions

You're going to come across some terminology and ideas in Revelation that you've probably never heard of—or at least don't know what they mean. You're not alone, so don't worry about that. But just so you'll have a fair idea of what these things are when you see them, here's a quick heads-up:

• *Symbolism.* First of all, you've got to understand that a lot of what you read in Revelation is not literal. A phrase or image may just *stand* for something. For example, when Jesus tells John to warn the church in Smyrna that they're going to face turmoil for "ten days" (2:10), it probably doesn't mean a real week and a half but rather some set amount of time. Also, when it says Jesus has "seven horns and seven eyes" (5:6), this is not a literal description of His physical appearance but a symbolic representation. We'll explain all this when we get there.

• *Storyline.* You might be coming to Revelation expecting it to flow chronologically, like a story that starts at a certain point in time and keeps moving toward the end. Revelation, though, is actually a combination of several different visions. Some of these sections describe the exact same events from a different perspective. At one point, in fact (chapter 12), it seems to stop the flow of events entirely and go way back in time. So don't approach Revelation thinking it's a step-by-step calendar of events. It's a good bit more complicated than that.

• *Tribulation.* If you take Revelation at face value, you'll see that a large part of the book (chapters 4–19) describes what's called the "great tribulation" (7:14) or the "hour of testing" (3:10). This is a unique period of time in history when the hardships faced by believers are going to be particularly intense. People disagree over when this will take place, but most everybody believes there will be some season of severe persecution as we get closer to Christ's second coming. Some believe the church will escape this by being "raptured." Some don't.

• *Millennium.* You heard this word a lot when we reached the year 2000 and entered the third millennium A.D. The one referred to in Revelation 20, however, is a particular period of 1,000 years when Christ will apparently reign on earth with His people. Again, there are various interpretations of this—some even saying that we're living in the symbolic era of the millennium *right* now—but many maintain that this is a future event just prior to the final judgment.

• *Seals, Trumpets, and Bowls.* These are a series of seven judgments apiece—seven particular calamities or disasters that will afflict the earth as an expression of God's anger against sin and to inspire the unsaved to repent. In the colorful language of Revelation, these judgments are described as the breaking of seven seals on a scroll, the blowing of seven trumpets, and the pouring out of seven wrath-filled bowls. Look at the outline following this section to see when these passages appear.

• *Antichrist.* You've almost certainly heard this fiendish title in reference to Revelation and the events of the end times. This evil opposite of Jesus—who claims to be God and leads the world in rebellion against heaven—will appear on the scene in chapter 13, only to wreak his hellish havoc and be canned at the end of chapter 19.

Revelation's Big Outline

1:1-20	John's Vision of Jesus
2:1–3:22	Letters to the Seven Churches
4:1–5:14	The Heavenly Throne Room
6:1–8:5	The Seven Seal Judgments
8:6–11:19	The Seven Trumpet Judgments
12:1–14:20	Satan, Antichrist, and False Prophet
15:1–16:21	The Seven Bowl Judgments
17:1–19:5	The Fall of Babylon
19:6-21	The Return of Christ
20:1-6	The 1,000-Year Reign
20:7-15	Final Judgment
21:1–22:21	New Heaven, New Earth

Revelation's Big Ideas

A REASON TO ENDURE. John's book appeals to the persecuted believers of his day—as well as the suffering Christians of every age—reminding us of the sure hope that awaits us if we'll just persevere, if we'll look past the immediate present, if we'll hang on to the end.

"The Devil is about to throw some of you into prison to test you, and you will have tribulation. . . . Be faithful until death, and I will give you the crown of life" (2:10).

THE LAMB AND THE LION. Revelation pictures Jesus as both the slaughtered Lamb and the Lion of Judah, the only One worthy to carry out His Father's will, the only One able to ride in victory over His enemies.

"'Look! The Lion from the tribe of Judah, the Root of David, has been victorious so that He may open the scroll and its seven seals.' Then I saw one like a slaughtered lamb" (5:5-6).

THE THRONE OF HEAVEN. This seat of authority, rule, and justice is mentioned forty times in Revelation. Its holy Occupant is the central focus of attention for all those in heaven. His Word and His very nature are frequently said to be "faithful and true."

"All the angels stood around the throne, the elders, and the four living creatures, and they fell on their faces before the throne and worshiped God" (7:11).

WORSHIP. Interspersed among the spectacular sights of heaven and the righteous judgments of our sinful earth are frequent, jubilant scenes of heaven-kissed worship and praise.

"There were loud voices in heaven saying: 'The kingdom of the world has become the kingdom of our Lord and of His Messiah, and He will reign forever and ever!'" (11:15).

THE SOVEREIGNTY OF GOD. This theological concept—referring to God's total, all-knowing, invincible control over history—gives the believer ultimate confidence that every one of the Lord's promises will be fulfilled. Satan can rattle and roar, but God will have the last word.

"Therefore rejoice, O heavens, and you who dwell in them! Woe to the earth and the sea, for the Devil has come down to you with great fury, because he knows he has a short time" (12:12).

THE GLORY OF HEAVEN. Revelation paints a picture of what our final dwelling place with God will be like. This is not wishful thinking or a wing and a prayer. This is the way it's going to be. Jesus has gone to prepare this place for us.

"He will wipe away every tear from their eyes. Death will exist no longer; grief, crying, and pain will exist no longer, because the previous things have passed away" (21:4).

THE TIME IS NEAR. No one knows when Christ is coming back. No one knows when death will be swallowed up in victory. But we do know that it's closer today than it was yesterday, and we need to be ready as if it were this afternoon. Jesus is coming soon!

"Look, I am coming quickly! Blessed is the one who keeps the prophetic words of this book" (22:7).

1:1-8 Prologue

Intro (verses 1-3)

Imagine waking up one morning, walking out on your back porch, closing your eyes to stretch, and when you open them—you're in a dream!

It's filled with monsters and fight scenes, with natural disasters and run-for-your-life adrenaline. You've never been so afraid, yet you've never felt so safe and protected . . . because every time you find yourself desperate to get away, you see a man you know to be Jesus, always there, always to the rescue.

That's what the Revelation is: a waking dream—but not just any dream. When John finally snapped out of it and found himself sitting alone again in his first-century world, he didn't have that early-morning feeling, like, "Whew! It was just a dream!" No, this dream was real—more real than the ground under his feet. It didn't come from eating too many wild strawberries the night before. It came directly from God.

God revealed "the words of this prophecy" to John for at least a couple of reasons:

1) *God wanted him to tell the people in the churches "what must quickly take place"* (verse 1). The time was near for some of these things to start happening, and He wanted His people to be ready, to recognize it, to expect what was coming.

2) *God also wanted to bless His people* (verse 3), to give them the opportunity to obey, to help them "keep" what was written here. Yes, this book is filled with words of "prophecy"—revelations about what was happening around them, predictions about what was (and is) still to come. But this book is not just information. It's a teaching to be heard and obeyed . . . and to enable us to be blessed by God for it.

SLAVES.
Though seen as cruel and unjust today, slavery was accepted throughout the ancient world and became a metaphor for unquestioning obedience to Christ.

ANGELS.
Unlike the TV and movie myths, real angels are created beings who serve God and carry out His will, not the living dead who come back to help people on earth.

Over and over again throughout this book, you'll see these two themes cropping up:

- "The time is near" for the end to come
- Blessing awaits those who are faithful to Him

John, the Friend of Christ (verses 4-5a)

John addressed his prophecy to the seven churches in Asia—an area which was under the occupying control of the Roman Empire. (Today, it's western Turkey.) But the words of this prophecy, far from being something that applied only to certain Christians in certain cities, had a universal message. Yes, it was intended for them, but it also applies to us.

This revelation, of course, is from God Himself. But notice that it came to John by way of all three persons of the Trinity:

1) The Father—"the One who is, who was, and who is coming"

2) The Son—"Jesus Christ, the faithful witness"

3) The Holy Spirit—"the seven spirits before His throne"

Look, too, at who the message is for. Even those of us who have a super-positive self-image probably don't realize the incredible worth and value we have in God's eyes.

- See how much He "loves us."
- See the sacrifice He's paid to "set us free from our sins."
- See how He's made us a "kingdom"—a never-ending nation with no boundaries, ruled by the King of kings.
- He's even made us "priests"—people with direct access to God.

Jesus, the Friend of Sinners (verses 5b-6)

We also get the point that while Revelation is filled with terrifying judgments for sinners and painful hardships for even the faithful, it's a message wrapped in worship (see the last part of verse 6).

You may be reading this book trying to figure out what's going to happen to you as the end approaches. That's understandable. But let's make it clear: this book is not so much about you as it is about God:

CITY CHURCHES.
As Christianity spread to new places in the years after Jesus' earthly life, those who believed in Him came together to form churches in the various towns. Unlike today, all believers considered themselves a part of the one, central church in their city.

SEVEN SPIRITS.
The number "seven" is a biblical symbol of perfection or completeness, like the seven days of creation and Israel's seven-day festivals. The "seven spirits," then, are a symbolic picture of the one, complete, perfect Holy Spirit.

- His justice—His absolute authority to make things right.
- His holiness—His perfect, blazing white purity, uniqueness, and separateness from created beings.
- His power—His undeniable control over all creation.
- His glory—His radiance, the riveting sight of His presence.
- His mercy—His willingness to forgive, to not hold us guilty.
- His love—His desire to have us near Him, to be welcomed.
- His everything—He is more than we can imagine. "Forever and ever. Amen."

Summary Statement (verses 7-8)

The second coming of Jesus, of course, is the grand finale of history and the great hope described in this book. He is the same One who came to Bethlehem as a baby and went to the cross to suffer and die for our sins. He burst from the tomb as the conqueror of death, and He will return again as both Judge and Deliverer.

"All the families of the earth will mourn over Him" when He comes (verse 7). Each of us will realize that we are the ones "who pierced Him"—not just the people of ancient Israel and not just the Romans who crucified Him. We are the ones whose sins drove the nails deep into His hands and feet. We are the ones whose guilty hearts pressed His head to His chest as He died.

Yet the unspeakable horror of our own role in Christ's suffering will quickly give way to the joy of His forgiveness. We will see Him, not captured by death or crippled by age and weakness, but fully alive, fully capable, fully in control of all that is to come.

KINGS OF THE EARTH.
Governments have authority to make their laws. Rulers have authority either to help or to harm their people. But ultimately, no king or leader has any authority at all unless God gives it to him (Romans 13:1), and those who reject His authority are fighting a losing battle (Psalm 2:10-12).

END-TIME PROPHECIES.
The imagery in verse 7 combines elements from two Old Testament prophecies: Daniel 7:13 (which talks about the "son of man" coming to reign) and Zechariah 12:10 (which pictures Him as the one "whom they pierced").

SECOND COMING.
Some people think the idea of Jesus' coming back to earth is nonsense. What they don't realize is that His delay is actually a sign of His mercy and patience, not His inability or weakness [2 Peter 3:9]. It's not for us to know when it will happen [Acts 1:7] but simply to be ready and waiting at all times [Luke 12:40].

ALPHA AND OMEGA.
These are the first and last letters of the Greek alphabet. This means Jesus is "the beginning and the end," eternal and in total control of history.

TRIBULATION.
This is a general sort of trouble, pressure, or suffering, which was especially acute for Christians living in John's day. Most people believe there will be a specific period of "great tribulation" to come in the last days [7:14].

Verse 8. Some people mistakenly believe that Jesus is somehow less than God, that He is a created being who hasn't always existed. They may say, "Well, He was born to Mary as a baby. Could God be born? Could God die?" But the Jesus who came to earth was Someone who was fully divine, while at the same time fully human. In His humanity, He had the same limitations as we do. He could feel pain, be tempted, and be confined to one place at a time. But in His deity, He was the living God, the one He had always been, "who is, who was, and who is coming." Yes, Jesus is eternal—past, present, and future.

He is coming." How does that make you feel? Scared? Worried? Not ready? Not sure? Pretty neat? What?

_____

_____

_____

1:9-20 John's Vision of Jesus

Sunday Surprise (verses 9-11)

John was living in exile on a prison island called Patmos (PAT-mus). He was by now an old man—almost certainly the last of the apostles still living at the time. With Rome elevating their emperor to near God-like status, Christian faith had become illegal. So, just as the emperor Nero had done in A.D. 64, the Roman government had again begun persecuting Christians, sometime around A.D. 95. This is most likely how John ended up here.

His commission to write the Revelation happened on "the Lord's day"—the first day of the week. Even though he was being held against his will, no one could keep him from being "in the Spirit" on his day of worship (verse 10). On this particular day, in this unexpected, desolate place,

Jesus had a special job and experience in store for him. He was to write the words of Christ to the churches in seven first-century cities. Here's the way to pronounce their names:

- Ephesus—EFF-uh-sus
- Smyrna—SMER-nuh
- Pergamum—PURG-uh-mum
- Thyatira—THIGH-uh-TIE-ruh
- Sardis—SAR-dis
- Philadelphia—just like the Pennsylvania one
- Laodicea—lay-AH-duh-SEE-uh

Is That You, Jesus? (verses 12-16)

For definitions of the "lampstands" (verse 12) and the "seven stars" (verse 16), let's wait till the next section. For now, let's just take a look at Jesus—in all His glory and blinding presence. Don't just read over these descriptions; take them slowly. Try to imagine what this sight looked like in John's eyes. The robe, the sash. The head, the hair. The feet, the voice.

Whenever you find yourself discouraged or disappointed, unable to pray or not feeling like following Christ, look into His face and imagine Him brighter than the noonday sun. Feast your eyes on the One who can help you "do all things" through His eternal might and strength (Philippians 4:13). He is powerful enough to meet your need, and worthy of your constant worship.

The "two-edged sword" protruding from His mouth (verse 16) sounds a little weird, almost gross. But like many things in Revelation, this is a word picture that illustrates a deeper reality. This sword is the truth of His Word. That's how the Scriptures are described in Hebrews 4:12.

Take a Letter (verses 17-20)

What does a "dead man" do? He lies motionless, cold, and still. He can't breathe. He can't think. He can't get up.

When John saw this magnificent vision of the risen Christ—the same Jesus he had known and lived with as a young man—he didn't have to think what to do. The awe

PATMOS.
This was a small, 6 x 10-mile island in the Aegean [uh-JEE-uhn] Sea, used by the Romans as an outpost for political exiles. According to tradition, John was sent there by the emperor Domitian [doh-MISH-un] in A.D. 95 for preaching the gospel and was released a year and a half later.

SON OF MAN.
This name for Jesus not only expressed His humanity but is also the title most associated with His return to earth and His judgment of humanity.

LAMPSTANDS.
A gold lampstand with seven branches extending upward [three to each side, one in the center] was a key worship element in Israel's history (Exodus 25:31-40). Also called a menorah [min-NOR-uh], it has become symbolic of the nation of Israel.

HADES.

This is the realm of the dead. The same word in Hebrew (the language of the Old Testament) is sheol, which is often described as a place of suffering but also as a netherworld for all those who have died.

SECRETS.

Jesus said in verse 20 that some of His terminology was a "secret." Truly, the book of Revelation is thick with imagery that seems strange and unknowable to us. Many people in our information age aren't comfortable with mystery and aren't happy with a God who's bigger than their brains. But ask them this: "If we were somehow able to figure out everything there is to know about God, what kind of a God would be left to worship?"

dropped him in his tracks . . . "like a dead man" (verse 17). Isn't it just like Jesus, though, to put His hand on John's shoulder and, without diminishing one light-flash of His glory, tell him, "Don't be afraid"? Jesus is full-on, eye-popping powerful, but He is also one hundred percent in love and in tune with His people.

The seven "lampstands" in this passage (verse 20) are said to represent the seven churches John will be writing to. Remember how Jesus said that we were to be "the light of the world" (Matthew 5:14-16)? The church shines the light of God's love in the darkness.

The "seven stars" are said to be the "angels" of the seven churches. This is a little confusing. Does every church have a guardian angel, the way people have angels watching over them? (Matthew 18:10). Perhaps. Another view is that Jesus was referring to the church's *pastors* as their "angels."

Verse 18. The body of Jesus—what is it like? What will He look like when we see Him coming again? His is a resurrected body, much like ours will one day become. His body is definitely divine and other-worldly (verses 14-15), but look—John can feel Jesus' hand resting on his shoulder (verse 17). He can hear His voice (verses 18-20). This is a body that experienced death (verse 18) yet is now alive "forever and ever." As Thomas and the other apostles could attest, Jesus still bore the wounds of crucifixion, even after coming back to life (John 20:27). He is full deity in a resurrected human body.

It's good to think of Jesus as being our Friend and Brother. But what's the danger of over-focusing on this, forgetting the aspect of Christ that made John nearly flat-line in front of Him?

_____

_____

_____

_____

Before reading and studying the letters to the seven churches, where Jesus gave sort of a report card on how they're doing, try to imagine what Jesus would say in a letter to your church or youth group. What would He single out for praise? What would He point to as a problem? How would you respond to it all? Would you feel the need to defend yourself? Would you accept it as a challenge? Would you be able to hear—one way or another—just how much Jesus loves your church?

2:1-6 The Letter to Ephesus

Good Report Card (verses 1-3)

Jesus had a lot of nice things to say about the Christians in Ephesus:

- They worked hard.
- They weren't quitters.
- They didn't put up with evil.
- They were on the watch for false teaching.
- They endured hatred without wearing down.

They possessed just about all the signs of a healthy and growing church. They probably would have had a really cool Web site and some cutting-edge, creative names for their various ministries. We might have even thought they were a little too good for us.

Bad Report Card (verses 4-7)

This church had one big problem, though, that dwarfed all the good stuff they were doing: they had lost their love for God (verse 4). This was no little thing. According to Jesus, this amounted to a nasty fall that required some major changes.

Did you ever come home from a retreat or summer camp on fire for the Lord? For a few weeks, you couldn't

APOSTLES.
These are messengers sent out under another's authority, specifically those who were sent out by the risen Christ as witnesses of His resurrection. They were a subset of the larger group of disciples, which carries more of the idea of a "student" or "follower."

NICOLAITANS.

Heretical group [Nik-oh-LAY-uh-tuhns] in the early church who taught immorality and idolatry. They are condemned in 2:6 and 2:15 for their practices in Ephesus and Pergamun. Thyatira apparently had resisted the false prophecy they preached [2:20-25]. The Nicolaitans have been linked to the type of heresy taught by Balaam [Numbers 25:1-2; 2 Peter 2:15], especially the pagan feasts and orgies that they apparently propagated in the first-century church.

TREE OF LIFE.

This life-giving source had a central place in the garden of Eden [Genesis 2:9] but was taken out of reach when Adam and Eve sinned [Genesis 3:22-24]. We're going to see it again, though, at the other bookend of the Bible [22:2].

get enough of Him. You prayed all the time. You worshiped even when it was nowhere near Sunday. But after a while, you could feel your enthusiasm slipping away, leaking out. You found yourself hanging around Him just because you knew you were supposed to.

Jesus once said that the whole law could be summed up in two commandments. The first and foremost of these is to love God with every part of your being (Mark 12:29-31). You can be doing a lot of good things. Your youth group can be taking mission trips and feeding the homeless and pulling in big crowds on Wednesday nights. But if you don't love Jesus—if you just sort of like Him—think how "far you have fallen" (verse 5).

The cure is pretty simple, although a long way from being easy: "Repent." Ask God for the ability to love Him again, to turn away from everything that hinders your affection for Him, and run back to Him with everything you've got. It doesn't mean you have to stay on a post-retreat high. (Nobody does that.) It just means you're always pursuing Him, desiring Him, loving Him.

Verse 5. In speaking to the church in Ephesus, what did Jesus mean when He threatened to "remove your lampstand from its place—unless you repent"? Does this mean a church can become unchristian and forfeit God's protection and blessing? Sure. Not every so-called church or Christian believes in or loves the God of the Bible. But we need to be re-e-e-ally careful about pronouncing this kind of judgment on anyone. As we'll see throughout chapters 2 and 3—and all of Revelation—Christ is jealously protective of His people. We give up on others a whole lot faster than Jesus does.

2:8-11 The Letter to Smyrna

Really Good Report Card

The Devil had his designs on this church—just as he does on you and yours. He wants you to suffer, to be afraid, to deny Christ and be killed. But Jesus told us not to "fear those who kill the body but are not able to kill the soul" (Matthew 10:28). Fear God instead—even with your life's blood—and you'll only have to die once (verse 11).

From all outward appearances, the church in Smyrna had been stripped of everything. This wasn't the popular place Ephesus seemed to be. The Christians in Smyrna were hated and mistreated by people claiming to do God's work every time they clamped down on them. But as God measured things, this church was "rich" in all the ways that mattered (verse 9)—in faithfulness, trust, and perseverance.

Most of us don't experience physical, life-threatening suffering for our faith. We know, however, that in eighty or more countries around the world today—like Sudan, China, and Vietnam—believers are being persecuted, imprisoned, and killed this very minute. Pray for them—and for us—because if anything, America is moving *closer toward* rather than *farther away* from this becoming an eventual reality here . . . on our shores.

It's not likely that you'll have to die for being a Christian. But would you be willing to? When you're thirty? Or forty? Or fifty? How does a person stay that committed to Christ?

_____

_____

_____

_____

POLYCARP.
It was in Smyrna, around A.D. 156, where this kindly, old bishop (POLLY-carp) was burned at the stake. According to the story, when the flames seemed to be avoiding him, a soldier stabbed him with a sword. But the blood spilling from the wound extinguished the fire. Undaunted, the murderers relit the wood and burned him to ashes.

RICH AND POOR.
God is fond of being the defender of the poor and helpless—and of declaring that the only wealth we should ever want is to be rich in faith (James 2:5).

SECOND DEATH.
This is spiritual death—final, irreversible separation from God.

SATAN.
Literally meaning "adversary" or "enemy," Satan is a created being who rebelled against God's authority and led other fallen angels in revolt [12:7-9]. He continues to oppose God's purposes in the world, though he is already defeated and merely biding his time [12:12].

ANTIPAS.
We're not sure who Antipas [ANN-tip-us] was or how he died, but tradition claims that he was roasted in a brazen bowl at the request of the emperor Domitian.

BALAAM AND BALAK.
Balaam [BAY-lum] was a Middle Eastern prophet who was urged by Balak [BAY-lack], king of Moab, to curse the invading Israelites for a fee—as though God was some genie who could be so easily manipulated. You may remember Balaam best for his run-in with a talking donkey [Numbers 22—24].

2:12-17 The Letter to Pergamum

Good Report Card (verses 12-13)

If someone asked you "where Satan lives" today, what would you say? Las Vegas? Amsterdam? Broadway? Down with the drunks and bums in the inner city? Up on some mountaintop where witches and Satanists pray to evil spirits?

In first-century Asia, apparently, one of the Devil's favorite haunts was Pergamum. It was the regional headquarters (so to speak) for worship of the Roman emperor, as well as a center for the worship of Greek gods and goddesses. "Satan's throne," which is mentioned in verse 13, may refer to one of the pagan altars situated there.

But there was a tough bunch of Christians living there, as well, who were "holding on to My name" even though it meant risking their skins. These were good people living in a hostile climate, and Jesus wanted them to know that He knew what they were up against.

Bad Report Card (verses 14-17)

"But I have a few things against you." For even though many of them were standing their Christian ground, some of them hadn't totally pulled away from their past or the other popular activities of the day.

In order to succeed in business in this city, it was customary to be part of organizations that met for meals in the temple halls. The meat they served at these feasts had usually been sacrificed to idols, and sexual immorality—then as it is now—was never too far from the party. Jesus didn't say that everybody in the church was doing this. But He included them all in the guilt . . . because they all knew about it and were turning a blind eye to it. We are not only at fault for the wrongs we commit but also for those we condone.

The church is a body, an interconnected group of believers. That's why it doesn't take but a small group of troublemakers to inject poison into the whole church. If there's an influencer in your youth group who's always negative about the student ministry, always critical of what God is doing, it affects everybody. It has to be dealt with and stopped.

Notice Jesus' commitment to "fight against them" (verse 16)—to preserve the purity, unity, and integrity of His church. He does it through the "sword"—the truth of His Word, which can be argued against from now till doomsday but never overcome.

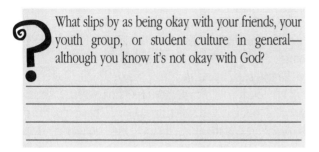

What slips by as being okay with your friends, your youth group, or student culture in general—although you know it's not okay with God?

_____

_____

_____

MANNA.
This refers to the food God gave each morning to the children of Israel as they wandered in the wilderness (Exodus 16:32-34). His "hidden manna" (verse 17) is Jesus, His Living Bread that came down from heaven (John 6:48-51).

WHITE STONE.
A white stone was often used in the ancient world as an admission ticket to a public festival. In this passage the "white stone" probably means being accepted by God (as opposed to being blackballed).

2:18-29 The Letter to Thyatira

Good Report Card (verses 18-19)
As in most of the other letters, Jesus had spotted a lot of good in this church:
- Love
- Faithfulness
- Service
- Endurance

Perhaps what made these traits even more noticeable was that the believers in this town were moving ahead with their faith. They were growing, developing, getting better at Christian living. It was obvious. You could see it.

NEW NAME.
It was a common biblical occurrence for those who were radically changed by God to be given a new name: Abram to Abraham, Jacob to Israel, Simon to Peter, Saul to Paul. Becoming a Christian made us, too, a new kind of person, worthy of a "new name."

Bad Report Card (verses 20-29)
Again, though—much like He had said to the church at Pergamum—Jesus found fault, not with what the church was doing, but with what it was willing to "tolerate" (verse 20).

Today, we have our own list of freedoms society begs us to tolerate: homosexuality, couples living together out-

JEZEBEL.
She was the wicked Phoenician queen of Israel's King Ahab [1 Kings 16:29-33], who hated Israel's God and sought to kill most of His prophets, particularly Elijah. She was eventually thrown from a window and trampled by horses in the street [2 Kings 9:30-37].

JUDGMENT.
Most people don't like to hear Jesus say, "I will give to each of you according to your works." But truthfully, we're all awaiting this reality, whether we feel comfortable with it or not. Even the saved, though forgiven of sin, will be "judged according to their works" [20:12], so . . . what we do and don't do on earth will matter in eternity.

MORNING STAR.
Jesus declared Himself to be the "Bright Morning Star" [22:16], and the light of His presence in our lives helps us understand the words and truths of Scripture [2 Peter 1:19]. Interestingly, Satan is also referred to in one place as the "shining morning star" who fell from heaven [Isaiah 14:12].

side of marriage, premarital sex, fornication, drug use (if it doesn't hurt anybody), and Eastern religions like Buddhism and Hinduism, the belief that all ways lead to God. Be careful what you accept as normal and okay. Even if you're committed to staying personally strong, you'll find yourself at odds with Jesus by what you accept.

Look what else you can learn about Jesus from this passage:

• *He is merciful* (verse 21). He gave the worst instigators of this faction "time to repent," although He knew they had no desire to change. His mercy is way more patient than ours.

• *He will punish and discipline* (verse 22-23). These are not idle threats, neither are they fits of holy revenge. These warnings of disease, disaster, and even death are not mere sentences against the guilty; they are protections against the spread of spiritual cancer.

• *He is all-knowing* (verse 23). Nothing slips past the careful scrutiny of Jesus' knowledge and awareness—neither the good nor the bad. He knows our "minds and hearts."

Revelation 3

3:1-6 The Letter to Sardis

Bad Report Card (verses 1-3)

Think of some people in your school or church who have a good reputation, but . . . well, you know for a fact they're not all they pretend to be. They may be known as super-nice, super-spiritual people, but you've seen them in plenty of situations where they weren't being either nice or spiritual. Their "works" are not "complete" (verse 2). They're just playing a part, acting out a faith they don't really possess.

Most of the Christians in Sardis must have been like that. They made sure they dressed to impress, but they neglected to notice that false fronts are more see-through than they realize.

Jesus doesn't go by reputation. He doesn't have to. But as we've seen several times already in Revelation, He also doesn't quit on His people—even those whose lives don't match their talk. There are few people we'd more like to see getting their just desserts than the fakes and phonies we know. But Jesus, though He's tough as nails and willing to back it up (verse 3), wants nothing more than for the half-hearted to be healed and made whole.

Good Report Card (verses 4-6)

One of the recurring themes in the Bible is the idea of a remnant—a piece of something left over, a surviving yet smaller portion of the whole. You've seen this in action on ball teams, for example—when just about all the players have quit trying except for one or two who continue to hustle. You've seen it when a group of friends are starting to get into trouble, but one of them decides to pull out and do what's right.

So as insincere as the people of Sardis were, there were still "a few people" (verse 4) who were living what they

SARDIS.
Once a great capital city, it had fallen twice to outside invaders—the Persians in 549 B.C. and the Romans in 188 B.C. Home of a temple to Artemis, the goddess of love and fertility, the city was rocked by an earthquake in A.D. 17.

LIKE A THIEF.
This is not the first time Jesus had warned His people to keep alert and anticipate His return. See His seriousness also in Luke 12:35-40 and Luke 21:34-36.

ETERNAL SECURITY.
One of the church's hotly debated doctrines is whether a person who's a Christian can fall away from grace and lose his salvation. Jesus made it really clear that He "will never erase" the names of those who have received eternal life [verse 5]. They "will never perish—ever! No one will snatch them out of My hand" [John 10:28]. The book of 1 John [especially 5:13] is also filled with passages on how we can "know" we have eternal life.

believed. And for this handful whose faith was genuine, Jesus promised some really nice things (verse 5)—just as He does for all His "victors":

• *White clothes.* White garments were worn as a symbol of victory after Roman triumphs, but these styles were nothing in comparison to the pure white fabric awaiting those of us who have received Christ's righteousness (Romans 5:17-19).

• An entry in the book of life. This listing of the saved is another frequent biblical device, appearing in Moses' writings (Exodus 32:32), in Jesus' teaching (Luke 10:20), in Paul's letters (Philippians 4:3), and several times in Revelation.

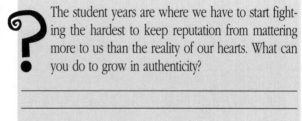

The student years are where we have to start fighting the hardest to keep reputation from mattering more to us than the reality of our hearts. What can you do to grow in authenticity?

_____

_____

_____

_____

3:7-13 The Letter to Philadelphia

Really Good Report Card

There's no doubt you feel at times as if your strength is "limited"—the same way the Christians in Philadelphia did (verse 8). But by keeping God's Word, not denying His name, and continuing to "endure" when times are tough on your faith, you'll experience Christ coming to your rescue. Life may seem like it's beating you up sometimes, but the One who loves you best (verse 9) will give you victory at last.

That's why we never need to be embarrassed of Christ. That's why we need to be proud of our church and an active part of its work and ministry. Life's hard enough. Don't toss out the main things that make it livable and give it hope.

KEY OF DAVID.
David, of course, was the greatest, most famous, most beloved king ever in Israel's history. This "key of David" gives Jesus the power to "open" the gates of God's heavenly kingdom for His people. It was mentioned before in Isaiah 22:22.

In addition to the ordinary, ongoing trouble we face today, Jesus indicated that an "hour of testing" was still to come (verse 10), apparently more widespread and severe than anything the world had ever known (Mark 13:19). He offered His people, though, the sure promise of permanence and protection—good reasons to "hold on to what you have" and never to give up. We have both His Word and His "name" on it (verse 12).

Verse 10. If you do your part "to endure," will God exempt you from going through any kind of "testing"? No. We know for a fact that Christians face difficult times—times when the pressure to conform is suffocating, when relationships are strained, when we're tempted to quit and not take this so seriously. When life gets intense like this, when the fire is hot, God reveals who His true believers are. They're the ones who don't quit. But there is apparently a time of future testing we're going to be spared from—either by our own deaths or through some other kind of divine deliverance. We know, at least, we'll ultimately be saved in the final hour.

SYNAGOGUE.
This was the name for the local meeting and assembly place of the Jewish people. It's close to what we'd think of as a church building. The "synagogue of Satan" was Jesus' name for those who were using religion for wicked purposes.

NEW JERUSALEM.
You'll hear more about this later in chapter 21, when this incredible, eternal city will come down "out of heaven from God" and become established on the new earth.

3:14-22 The Letter to Laodicea

Lukewarm Report Card

You've got your cell phone. You've got your music. You've got your weekend plans. You've got your spending money. You've got your friends and your family. Put it all together, and you can kid yourself into believing you won't be needing God for at least another week and a half.

The folks in Laodicea were a lot like some of us. They pretty much had everything they could want or need. And as it almost always does, this smug self-sufficiency had leaked over into their relationship with Christ. They were bored with Jesus, easily offended, full of excuses. They were like some of the people you know in your youth group who don't care about anything, who have no passion, who go months without praying or reading their Bibles.

JESUS' DIVINITY.
We mentioned this back in chapter 1, but it's important enough to repeat it: Jesus is God. There was never a time when He didn't exist. His claim of being the "Originator of God's creation" (verse 14) places Him before all things and does not make Him in any way a second-level member of the Trinity. He is the real thing, one with the Father and the Spirit.

REFINING.
This is the process of reducing a metal down to its purest state and eliminating its impurities. The Bible translates this in spiritual terms, referring to the way God uses hard times to burn away the bits of unfaithfulness we've picked up over the years [Zechariah 13:9].

DISCIPLINE.
Two other Scriptures that talk about the Father's loving reasons for disciplining us are found in Proverbs 3:11-12 and Hebrews 12:5-11.

So while they thought of themselves as being "rich"—as being at least as good as the next person—Jesus used some less appealing adjectives to describe the state of their hearts: "wretched, pitiful, poor, blind, and naked" (verse 17).

Jesus wasn't leaving these people without help and hope, though. He never does. He held out to them the "gold" of true Christian contentment, the "white clothes" of God-dependent purity, and the "ointment" of spiritual honesty (verse 18).

Then, in one of the most well-known passages in all the Bible (verse 20), He reminded them how patiently but persistently He was waiting for them, eager to be received into their lives, hungry for their time and attention, and serious about ushering them into the blessing of living for Him with all their hearts.

Verse 15. Do you get why Jesus would say He'd rather us be "cold" than "lukewarm"? You can understand why He'd want us to be "hot"—on fire for God. But it seems as though being so-so—"lukewarm"— would at least be better than being frozen solid! The trick in figuring this out is not to think of "cold" as being bad but like an icy swig of spring water on a summer day. "Hot" is good. "Cold" is good. "Lukewarm" is bad—like a flat soda or a weak tea. Laodicea was a place that had trouble with their water supply. Instead of having naturally cold drinking water or hot, steamy bath water, they had this bland, lukewarm stuff that wasn't good for anything. Jesus wants us to be turned on for Him—coolly refreshing to the thirsty, sizzlingly soothing to the hurting—not the same room temperature as everybody else.

> What usually precedes a season of "lukewarm"-ness for you? What does it usually take for you to break out of it?

_____
_____
_____

A Break in the Action

Before we move to chapter 4, which begins the second of four visions in the book of Revelation, make sure you remember this from this first section: Jesus loves His church.

The Bible says that Jesus loves His people so much, He "gave Himself for her" (Ephesians 5:25). Even now, He continues to be the head of the church, (Ephesians 4:15), to place faithful leaders and pastors over us, and (as we have seen) to fight to protect us.

Yes, He knows both the good and the bad about us. He confronts us when we need a kick in the pants. But He does it all to purify and unite us—to make us more effective servants, to enable us to glorify Him and be blessed in the process.

So don't let yourself get caught up in badmouthing the church, running down your leaders, or living in such a way that you bring disgrace on it and on Him. Remember how much Jesus loves and will protect His church. And make sure you love it, too!

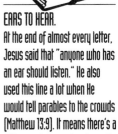

EARS TO HEAR.
At the end of almost every letter, Jesus said that "anyone who has an ear should listen." He also used this line a lot when He would tell parables to the crowds (Matthew 13:9). It means there's a difference between hearing and listening, between hearing and obeying. The reason why some people don't listen to Him is because He doesn't say what they want to hear.

> What do you find the most convicting to you in these letters to the seven churches? What do you find the most encouraging?

_____
_____
_____

Revelation 4

4:1-6 In the Throne Room

Change gears. Now we're in heaven—sort of like "mission control" for everything that's about to take place on earth. And suddenly, out of nowhere, Jesus speaks again "like a trumpet"—pounding with more window-pounding bass than the loudest boom box you've ever heard. John felt it in his feet, in his stomach, in his wisdom teeth. When he turned around, there was the throne—the throne of God! How intimidating do you think that would be? You know what it's like, probably, to be sent to the principal's office. Maybe you know what it's like to stand before the judge in traffic court. Multiply that sinking feeling about ten thousand percent, and you're still nowhere close to the shocking sensation John must have felt in this scene.

Look at what a throne it is! Fashioned out of precious stones, surrounded by a glistening rainbow, and shooting out sparks of thunder and lightning, it rises in front of a crystal sea. Try to picture it! And realize that these word images—as spectacular as they are—can't come anywhere close to describing it.

Verse 4. The "24 elders" seem to be some kind of heavenly beings, although some believe they are simply representative of believers who have died in Christ. If indeed they are another class of creature than humans, they verify that there are other beings in existence besides us. But by their worship and subjection to God, they demonstrate that God is in control of all that exists. There are no aliens on par with His mind, no other worlds with other Gods, no UFOs. God has made and identified everything there is. He is the one and only, the supreme.

JEWELS.
Jasper is a green, quartz-like stone, though it can be red, yellow, or brown. Carnelian is much the same, only more of a dark red. Emerald is a gem of the bright green variety.

LIVING CREATURES.
First seen in an Old Testament prophetic vision (Ezekiel 1:4-14), these cherubim (Ezekiel 10:20) are a class of winged angels. Their four faces represent the four classes of creation: lion (wild beasts), calf (domestic beasts), man (humanity), and eagle (birds).

4:7-11 All-Out Worship

If we were to sing the same song over and over again, we'd get tired of it in a hurry. But if we truly saw God as clearly as we should, we'd realize what an honor it is to worship Him. We might only have one song to sing, but we'd sing the fiftieth verse with as much heart and passion as the first.

That's what these "living creatures" are doing . . . "day and night" (verse 8). These ones who live closest to the throne—who (you'd think) might be bored with all this by now—cannot stop worshiping the One "who lives forever and ever" (verse 10).

We don't have room here to explain what all their unusual bodily characteristics mean, as described in verses 7 and 8, but the point is this: these angelic wonders are awe-inspiring in their presence and power.

Think about this, too: If these created beings can strike shock and surprise in our hearts, just imagine the dazzling divinity of the One who thought them up and spoke them into existence!

Verse 10. Does it ever strike you, when God is basking in the praise of His people, that it seems a little proud of Him to demand our worship? Maybe you've never said it out loud, but . . . shouldn't He handle praise more the way we know we're supposed to—by deflecting it, downplaying it, aw-shucks-ing it? No, unlike us, God is in a unique position to seek glory for Himself. This is not a matter of pride on His part; this is just something He rightly deserves. The reason we can't receive unbridled praise is because we couldn't do anything unless God gave us bodies and a heartbeat, brains and a blood supply. He, on the other hand, is self-supporting perfection, complete power, everything He says He is—and more! He has no rival. When we worship Him, we're just repeating the truth.

WORSHIP WORDS.
Many of the terms found in verse 11 also appear in some of our hymns and praise songs, so we need to know what they mean when we sing them. Glory tries to capture the radiance and shining majesty of God's presence. Worthy describes God's unique, exclusive right to receive our honor and worship. He is everything He claims to be. He deserves all praise.

LORD AND GOD.
Domitian [doh-MISH-un], one of the cruelest of all the first-century Roman emperors, wanted all his subjects to acknowledge him by this title—"Lord and God"—which is ascribed to its only real Owner in verse 11.

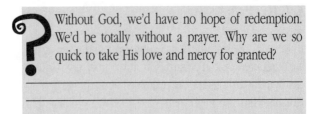

Without God, we'd have no hope of redemption. We'd be totally without a prayer. Why are we so quick to take His love and mercy for granted?

_____

_____

_____

_____

Revelation 5

SCROLL.
A scroll containing the words of God's law and teaching was supposed to be one of the Israelite king's treasured, take-everywhere possessions (Deuteronomy 17:18-20).

SEVEN HORNS.
This sounds kind of monstrous to us, but "seven," you remember, is the prophetic number of perfection, and "horns" are a biblical symbol of strength (Daniel 7:7). These "seven horns," then, simply stand for Jesus' complete power.

5:1-7 The Lamb Takes the Scroll

When John saw the scroll "in the right hand of the One seated on the throne" and discovered how desperately it needed to be opened—and how powerless anyone was to do it—the Scripture says he "cried and cried" (verse 4).

Have you ever felt that way? Maybe your parents were going through a divorce, or one of your friends was critically injured in an accident. There was nothing you could do to make things better. You prayed, you cried, knowing that only Jesus could do anything about this situation. The words spoken to John in verse 5 tell it all: "Stop crying. Look!" Jesus is here. And Jesus can help.

Scrolls were the books of the ancient world. They were made of long pieces of papyrus glued together, then spooled up on both ends and unrolled as the person read. The scroll talked about in this chapter, though, was unique in several ways:

• *The writing was on both sides of the paper*, unlike most scrolls, but similar to the prophetic one mentioned in Ezekiel 2:10.

• *It was sealed with seven seals*, but even as these seals are about to be snapped over the next few chapters, they won't reveal the whole contents of the scroll, just the opening edge.

• *No one could open it* except the One who had been given authority by the Father.

Verse 5-6. How can these verses describe Jesus as both a "lion" and a "lamb" at the same time? Well, first of all, these pictures John had of Jesus are not to be taken literally. They are both needed to represent His nature and character. He is the "Lion" descended from one of Israel's earliest ancestors (Genesis 49:9). He is the "Root" because He grew from the family tree of King David (Isaiah 11:10). He is the "slaughtered lamb" because He was sacrificed on the cross. He is all of these things all at once. But it's not as though He's morphing into the form of an animal or appearing like some sort of murky hologram.

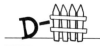

TRINITY.

We've talked about the Trinity already—the fact that God is three persons (Father, Son, and Spirit) in one, united whole. This is hard to understand, especially when you see the Lamb coming to take the scroll from "the One seated on the throne" (verse 7). They seem so separate here. But those who claim we worship three Gods are missing the point that the Father, Son, and Spirit do have distinct roles, while still maintaining their central unity.

5:8-10 Prayers of the Saints

Have you ever experienced times when praying and worshiping and being blown away by God's love and greatness is not just a chore and a have-to, but a that's-all-I-want-to-do?

That's the way it is every time you turn around in the book of Revelation. You find yourself at another worship service. In this one, in fact, you can literally sense yourself participating, as the twenty-four elders bring out their "gold bowls" filled with "the prayers of the saints" (verse 8). That means you—your prayers, your expressions of worship—being presented to the Lamb!

Every time you pray, both your words and the genuine devotion of your heart rise up to God like a sweet-smelling offering, like the perfume curling from a stick of incense. Your prayers matter! They make a difference! They are a pleasant aroma floating through the halls of heaven.

5:11-14 Can't Get Enough Worship

REDEMPTION.
To redeem someone in biblical times meant to pay whatever price was needed to buy the release of a convicted criminal. God sent Jesus to pay our price, to set us free, to give us redemption from our sins.

AMEN.
This refers to something that is absolutely certain, one hundred percent true and valid. After taking in this amazing spectacle of God's glory and Christ's worthiness, the crowd's "Amen" simply meant, "Let it ever be so!"

THOUSANDS.
The Old Testament background to this scene is found in Daniel 7:10, where "ten thousand times ten thousand" stood before the throne in Daniel's prophetic vision.

What's more, it's not just people like us who are represented there. This "kingdom" of God is inhabited by people of "every tribe and language" (verse 9), those He has redeemed from Canada and Cameroon and California and the Caribbean—from every nook and cranny of creation—into one, united family of "priests" and praisers. (No more cliques and categories. Won't that be great?)

Even bigger than that, the cries of blessing aren't just coming from the earth but from "every creature in heaven, on earth, under the earth, on the sea . . ." (verse 13). God's people and creatures from all over the place are part of this thing—"countless thousands, plus thousands and thousands" (verse 11)—way bigger than any crowd you've ever seen at an outdoor concert or a Super Bowl. Think in terms of square miles of people, all in one place, lost in worship and belting it out just as loudly as they can. That's the idea of heaven.

> Here we are, standing at the edge of the end, waiting to see what's about to take place. Why is worship, rather than worry, such an appropriate response to the way this makes us feel?
>
> _____
>
> _____
>
> _____

Revelation 6

6:1-2 Seal #1—Military Power

The mood is rich with anticipation. And fear? Maybe. But by approaching the dreadful prospects of the seven seals with worship and adoration, those in heaven show us that when we're convinced of ultimate victory, when we're fully trusting in the Lord, even the scary stuff can be endured by God's grace and power.

So here we go—not knowing exactly what we're getting into, but knowing that God is going with us.

In biblical, prophetic language, the number four tends to represent the earth. These first four seals, then, seem to tell us about things that will happen (and are already happening) on earth as we march toward the end of time.

Most people believe the "white horse" represents military power and conquest—and not always the best kind of power or the most popular sort of "victor" (verse 2). Domination by one person or by one group of people almost always results in less than ideal conditions for those who must live under their heel and fist.

HORSEMEN.
There's a very similar picture of these four horsemen in Zechariah 6:1-8.

WHITE HORSE.
It's easy to get the white horse of 6:2 confused with the one Jesus will ride down from heaven in 19:11. The One who wears not one crown (verse 2) but "many crowns" (19:12) will not be coming to begin a series of human horrors but to ride in victorious defeat over all His enemies.

6:3-4 Seal #2—War

In an age of terrorist attacks and war conflicts in Iraq and elsewhere, our generation is aware again of what war means and costs and feels like. If you know someone who's serving in battle, or if someone from your local area has been killed while deployed in action, you know better than most how difficult, fearful, and demanding wartime can be.

The second rider is atop a blood-red horse, which undeniably represents war and violence. War, of course, is an ugly business, even when fought for the noblest causes. It has been a part of human history for as long as we've existed. And as long as we're here, it always will. The fire, the sword, the "slaughter"—these are all a big part of the news every day, and we can expect even more as the end approaches.

6:5-6 Seal #3—Poverty

The "balance scale" in the hand of the third rider apparently speaks of poverty and want. Again, just like war and conquest, poverty continues to be a huge scourge on the human family. From the bloated bellies of third-world babies to the homeless drifters living off handouts in the inner city, we're all too familiar with the faces of hunger and need.

To make matters even more depressing: when the price of bare necessities—like "wheat" and "barley" in Bible times—just keeps going up, when a full day's work doesn't earn you enough to eat on, the problem of poverty is certain to get worse and worse.

DENARIUS.
One denarius [dih-NEHR-ih-uhs] was a small silver coin equal to a day's wage for a common laborer.

WHEAT AND BARLEY.
These were bread-making staples of the ancient Near East—barley in particular being the common food of the poor. Olive oil and wine, on the other hand, were more naturally found in the homes of the wealthy. Verse 6 indicates that some people don't mind if food is hard for the poor to come by, as long as the rich have everything they want.

Have you ever thought about what it would be like to really suffer and be in need? How do you think you would react to that? What would that do to your faith in God?

_____

_____

_____

_____

6:7-8 Seal #4—Death

Instead of thinking of "pale green" as a color that might look nice with your eyes or match the wallpaper in your bathroom, think instead of the gray-green skin of a human corpse. This horseman is specifically identified as "Death"—and his old pal "Hades" (the grave, the dwelling place of the dead) is always close behind him.

A lot of people's lives—not all, but many—have been touched by these four disasters throughout history and in our present day: military might, war, hunger, and untimely death. Even more, of course, will face them in the future. John communicated this by mentioning the one-fourth portion of the earth who are set to fall under "famine," "plague," and other such scourges (verse 8).

Think AIDS. Think E. coli. Think way bigger than 9-11, like on a worldwide scale. Out of 6 billion people living on the planet, if this one-fourth gauge is anywhere near being literal, think 1.5 billion people losing their lives.

COSMIC TERROR.
A period of widespread death and destruction was prophesied often in the Old Testament. Take a look at Isaiah 2:12-22, for example.

Verse 8. When God is said to give "authority" to the four horsemen to go out and work their distress, does that make Him responsible for death and suffering? He could stop it if He wanted to, couldn't He? Yes. And He does prevent more of it than we know—much more of it than we sinful humans deserve. But although He allows it to occur for reasons known only by His holy will, He maintains the power to withhold it from going any farther than He gives it permission. These bitter enemies are not at liberty to do whatever they want with us. God is fully aware of the pain and evil in our world, but He is not the cause of it.

6:9-11 Seal #5—Martyrs

A change in perspective happens here. Instead of the earth being the focus of attention, all eyes are now on a group of people already in heaven—the martyrs—those who were killed for holding to their faith in God.

But the time of suffering on earth is not yet over. The Lord knows that many more will be killed for their Christian testimony . . . and He knows just how many that number will be (verse 11).

So do you want to know what would happen to you if you were to die today as a believer? This passage gives us some clues. You would be in heaven with Christ. You

THE DEAD.
You'll come across a lot of different beliefs about what happens to people after they die. Some believe we go into some sort of soul-sleep while waiting for final judgment. Others believe we hang out in purgatory, kind of a holding tank on our way to either heaven or hell. Verse 10 as well as other Scriptures, however, indicate that believers depart to "be with Christ" (Philippians 1:23), while the unsaved go immediately into "torment" (Luke 16:22-23).

REST.
The Bible uses this refreshing word to describe why Christians have freedom both over death and after death (Hebrews 4:8-11). It's not a rest that amounts to laziness, but the feet-up feeling of having done your best and deserving a chance to relax.

would not be able to be tempted by evil, but you would know it was still happening on the earth (verse 10), and you could pray to God for Him to work His will in these situations. Time would pass, indicated by their being told to wait "a little while longer" (verse 11). You would also be in some sort of recognizable form or body (verse 9), but this would apparently be an intermediate state until you took on your full, resurrected body at the "first resurrection" (20:6).

How about that? Pretty sharp, huh?

 Verse 10. Notice that these martyrs are aware of what's happening on earth and continuing to pray, asking God to punish the wicked for their murderous crimes. Does that sound very godly—asking Him to pay people back for the bad things they've done? What ever happened to turning the other cheek (Matthew 5:39)? This kind of request is allowed, however, (see Psalm 58, for example)—not to seek our own revenge, not to delight at another's misfortune—but to want to see God's cause defended. "Then people will say, 'Yes, there is a reward for the righteous! There is a God who judges on earth!'" (Psalm 58:11).

6:12-17 Seal #6—Cosmic Calamity

There are some things we've always counted on. Spring following winter. Snow on the Rockies. The World Series in October. But in preparation of the "day" of God's "wrath" (verse 17), the sun's not going to come up one morning. The moon, the stars—even the ground underneath our feet—are all going to lose their predictable qualities. People not only are going to feel out of control, but actually be out of control. Suddenly and without warning, what we've always thought of as normal and routine will cease to be.

SACKCLOTH.
Similar in feel to a burlap bag, this coarse, itchy garment (usually made of goat or camel hair) was worn as a sign of mourning, guilt, or anguish.

Can anybody stop an earthquake? Can kings? Military commanders? Presidents? World leaders? Internet moguls? Big business CEOs? The rich and powerful? Truly, for those who thought they had life by the tail, this change of plans will come as a shocking, sobering surprise. Unbelievers who, as long as life was going their way, didn't give God credit for having much power, will know in an instant just how wrong they were. The justice the martyrs had pled for in verse 10 will come raining down in big buckets of fear and falling stars. "And who is able to stand?" (verse 17).

Won't we be glad then that we put our trust in the worthy One?

This chapter talks about some serious stuff. How does this change the way you view current world events? Does it make you react any differently to tragedy?

_____

_____

_____

_____

DAY OF THE LORD.
This was an Old Testament synonym for God's judgment and deliverance (Amos 5:18), which the New Testament writers deepened to mean Christ's final coming—the ultimate judgment day, the "day of their wrath" (verse 17).

Revelation 7

All right, things have gotten scary at this point. The sun's gone out like a birthday candle. The sky has fallen in. Every time we've complained about having a bad day, we were wrong. THIS is a bad day!

So God interrupted John's dream of destruction to bring him and his readers (including us) a word of encouragement: "Yes, it's going to get bad before it gets better, but I promise: I will take care of you." That's the theme of this whole chapter.

7:1-8 Interlude

Okay, Hold It (verses 1-3)
You were expecting the seventh seal to be broken at this point, right? What we think and what God thinks, however,

SEAL.
Many property owners in biblical times had some sort of stamp that could be inked or pressed into clay, marking their possessions as their own. It was like their signature or a brand label.

FOREHEAD MARK.
There's an earlier prophecy that parallels the scene from verse 3, where those with some kind of ID mark were spared from God's righteous anger (Ezekiel 9:4-6). You also see this when the blood on the doorposts protected the Israelites when God struck down the firstborn of every family in Egypt—the first Passover (Exodus 12:13).

TRIBES.
These were family lines dating back to the sons of Jacob (Genesis 49:28). Every Jewish person—even up until Jesus' time—was known as coming from one of these families, from one of the twelve tribes of Israel.

TWELVE.
Twelve is a common biblical number: the twelve apostles, for example. Even multiples of twelve have special significance, like the twenty-four elders (4:4) and these twelve thousand members (12 x 10) from each of the twelve tribes of Israel.

are not always the same thing. Revelation clearly shows that God is in charge, that the flow of this very day and the pattern of earth's final days are all in His good care and keeping. And all of us who are believers are better off that way!

So at this unexpected interlude, something else unusual happens. We see "four angels" who've been standing at the "four corners of the earth," keeping things from getting any worse than they are. These heavenly beings have both the authority and ability "to harm the earth and the sea"—what power! But before they are turned loose, God dispatches another angel—one who has a different, more urgent duty—to postpone the four angels' actions temporarily.

Protection must come before destruction. God's people are not exempt from life, but we are always under His watchful eye and overseen by His strong and mighty angels.

A Great Day for 144K (verses 4-8)

Among those God has promised to set apart for protection are these "144,000" John talks about in verse 4. Some people (like the Jehovah's Witnesses) interpret this to mean everybody in their little cult or religious group—as if no one else has any chance of seeing heaven.

The 144,000 refers to believing Jews—just like it says—not an exact number of them, but all who are trusting the Messiah for salvation. Every other time in the New Testament when the word "Israel" is used, it always refers to the Jewish people. Romans 11 also speaks in very plain terms about some of the Jews coming to faith in Christ.

So while we can expect life to get even harder on true believers as the end draws near—Jews and otherwise—we can also count on "the seal of the living God" (verse 2) to protect us from the threat of total destruction. His seal basically says to the angels and everybody else, "You can't touch that!"

7:9-17 Believers Who Made It Through

Think about a time when you spent a month or more not knowing if you were going to make it through a really bad situation. Maybe it was a problem in your family. Or an ongoing misunderstanding with somebody at church. Or the last six weeks of chemistry class. Think about someone who's been kidnapped or held hostage, but who is finally rescued or escapes from the brutality and abuse. When you finally come through it, when you can breathe again, when it feels like the clouds have finally parted for you, the relief is really sweet, isn't it?

The people described in this passage have just come through the fire, "out of the great tribulation" (verse 14). There are a lot of them—so many that no one can number them all (verse 9). And they are coming into heaven in waves, in droves, having been brutalized for being believers (17:6). They are dressed all in white, their souls purified by the cleansing, forgiving "blood of the Lamb" (verse 14).

They've been starved, mistreated, tortured, and burned at the stake. But the Lord has promised them a place without hunger, thirst, sorrow, or danger (verse 16). They've been in the fight of their lives on earth. Now they're being rewarded big-time in heaven.

PALM BRANCHES.
These appear only twice in the New Testament—here in this scene of heavenly worship, and earlier at Jesus' triumphal entry into Jerusalem a week before His death (Palm Sunday). Palm branches were a symbol of beauty, prosperity, and joy— the equivalent of balloons at a party.

ONE WAY.
The ones in white, the ones standing before the throne, are there "for this reason" (verse 15): they have been redeemed by the Lord Jesus. In our current culture, this statement sounds narrow-minded and arrogant. But the truth is this: if it weren't "for this reason," there would be no reason at all. If it weren't for Christ, there would be no hope.

Verse 14. One of the big questions of Revelation is this: Is the "great tribulation" a specific, future period of intense suffering for Christians, or is it just the long history of persecution that's been happening ever since John's day? Is it still to come, or are we in it right now? People who hold to the end-time variety of tribulation believe this verse refers to a huge influx of souls coming into heaven all at once or in a short period of time—those who are "raptured" or taken up to heaven the way the Left Behind books describe it. People who prefer the more general interpretation see this as the steady, age-old stream of the murdered, mistreated, and martyred.

Describe how it feels when you've hung tough through a long ordeal . . . without giving up or giving in. What would have happened if you hadn't endured? What would it have cost you?

_____

_____

_____

_____

Revelation 8

We interrupt this scene of white robes and palm branches to return you to earth, to the scene of some "breaking" news. As we reported to you in the last chapter, the seventh and final seal, which seemed ready to be broken at the end of chapter 6, was momentarily delayed. It does appear now, however, that the seal is about to be broken. If we're reading it right, this will begin a series of "trumpet" judgments (chapters 8–9).

These warnings and punishments can be interpreted two ways:

• *Re-runs.* Some scholars believe that the seals, trumpets, and bowls are the same exact seven judgments, described three different times, only in deeper levels of detail.

• *Chronological.* Others believe the seven seals, trumpets, and bowls describe different events, one following the other. This seems to be the most straightforward reading of it.

Or perhaps the answer lies somewhere between the two, with the seals and the trumpets being separate judgments, but the bowls being a repeat—a different twist on the trumpets.

Whichever way you slice it, one thing is for sure: this incredible storyline means bad news for the unbelievers and a wonderful wrap-up for the redeemed.

8:1-2 Seal #7—Another Set of Judgments

Passing Out the Trumpets (verses 1-2)

You've probably experienced what they call "the silence before the storm," when there's a noticeable hush outside, a stillness you can feel. You also get this feeling when you're watching a suspense thriller. Some main character can be walking through a dark room or passageway. The music is low. The silence is eerie. It's quiet. Too quiet. Something's about to come busting out—you just know it!

Now you're in the mood of Revelation 8. A moment of silence. Then . . . pow! All heaven breaks loose! As the seventh seal is peeled back, it reveals "seven angels" with "seven trumpets" (verse 2). Starting with verse 7, we'll see what all these trumpets are for.

ALTAR.

This place of sacrifice [the same as the one mentioned in 6:9, as well as 9:13] is like the gold altar of incense found in Exodus 40:5. No longer is it used to offer the blood of animals to pay for sins, but to represent the "once for all" sacrifice of the Lamb [Hebrews 9:28], which now gives us access to the holy place of God.

More Prayers of the Saints (verses 3-6)

Notice again how prized and powerful your prayers are in heaven. I mean, God is listening! Your prayers really do go places.

It is so easy to think that praying is optional. The Devil loves to try convincing us of that. But prayer is for so much more than the dinner table and the start of a church service. Prayer is for the bathroom sink and the driver's seat. It's for the living room sofa and the lawn mower. It's for the walk to class and the middle of the day.

Back in 5:8, remember, we saw the gold bowls filled with the sweet aroma of our prayers. Then in 6:9-10, we saw the martyred saints pleading at the altar for God to take revenge on the ones who took their lives.

Now in verse 4, all of these heartfelt prayers—both theirs and ours—are combined into a smoky mix of sweet-smelling intercession that drifts up into "the presence of God." When the angel sends a shovelful of this blazing brew hurtling toward the earth (verse 5), the trumpeters wet their lips for God's holy answer to begin . . . in fire and fury.

Does it surprise you to see angels doing this kind of

TRUMPETS.

These were used in ancient Israel to summon the people to attention, as well as to announce a battle or a solemn emergency [Joel 2:1].

PRAYER.

Even Jesus, the Son of God, was a habitual person of prayer. His disciples saw this and recognized the difference between their prayer passion and His. That's why they asked Him to "teach us to pray" (Luke 11:1). See how Jesus answered them in Luke 11:2-13.

hard, heavy work? You'll see them throughout this chapter—and throughout this book—always following God's commands and in various capacities of service. They are not wimpy featherweights who just strum their harps and make sure the clouds are nice and fluffy. These are mighty members of God's heavenly regiments, and their work is serious business.

Where is prayer on your list of priorities? What would be different about your relationship with Christ if you let prayer become a bigger part of your day?

_____

_____

_____

_____

8:7 Trumpet #1—Hail and Fire

Have you ever been in a classroom where everybody's talking and laughing and taking advantage of the teacher's good nature? For a little while she tries nicely to get everybody to behave, but nobody listens. Then when everything's finally gotten way out of hand, she yells out, "I've had enough of this!" and slams a book down hard on the desk.

The room goes quiet. NOW she has your attention.

These trumpet judgments are sort of like that. Up until now, God has been nudging people toward repentance, punishing sin and seeking repentance through (mainly) low-level forms of discomfort. But when "a third of the earth" is on fire—quickly becoming both treeless and grassless—you don't have to be a genius to see that He means business.

EXODUS PLAGUES.

These trumpet judgments have a lot of similarities to the disasters God rained on the ancient Egyptians in the book of Exodus (chapters 7–11)—fiery hail, darkness, locusts, rivers turned to blood, death.

Oh, and one more thing: just as we saw with the first four "seals" in chapter 6, these first four "trumpets" describe afflictions that God will rain on the *earth*—on the environment, on nature. With the start of chapter 9 and the fifth trumpet, you'll see the difference in perspective. Be watching for that.

8:8-9 Trumpet #2—Meteorite Tidal Wave

When we think about God's judgment of sin, we typically think just about His judgment of people. But did you know that the earth, too, has suffered the curse of Adam's sin? Did you know that "the whole creation has been groaning" with the aftershocks of the Fall, the introduction of sin onto planet Earth? (Romans 8:22). So it's not without reason that the earth is being judged in this way, taking the blows of God's righteous anger, so that one day it can be replaced by something new and better (chapter 21).

At the blast of the second trumpet, something like a gigantic meteorite cannonballs into the sea. The fish don't stand a chance. Neither do the ocean vessels, even huge ones like aircraft carriers, capsized in the resulting tidal wave. "A third" of the sea life is killed—think about that!—setting off a huge environmental crisis, not to mention the economic collapse caused by the inability to transport goods by ship.

SIGNS AND WONDERS.
This is not the first time God has warned of "wonders in the heaven and on the earth: blood, fire, and columns of smoke" (Joel 2:30).

8:10-11 Trumpet #3—Contaminated Rivers

More fireworks! Again, a huge hot-rock pounds the earth, this time infecting the freshwater rivers and springs, contaminating the drinking water supply and killing off who-knows-how-many people in the process.

The only thing we could compare this to would be something like the explosion of the nuclear reactor at Chernobyl in 1986, which exposed millions of people to deadly radiation and contaminated untold acres of farmland, rivers, and other natural resources. The effects of this disaster really did reach around the world—into the nearby Nordic countries and across the continent of Europe—and has all but destroyed the livelihood of the people in Belarus.

The third trumpet, however, will make Chernobyl look like nothing.

WORMWOOD.
This Middle Eastern plant was so well-known for its bitterness, it became a symbol for all the distasteful results of sin. It has become famous in our day as the name of the junior demon in C. S. Lewis's Screwtape Letters.

8:12 Trumpet #4—Darkening of the Sun

NATURAL DARKNESS.
When Mount Saint Helens volcano erupted in 1980, a mushroom shaped blast of gray ash belched into the air and plunged the eastern Washington region and beyond into a day of darkness, while the debris drifted around the earth several times before disintegrating. See, this global destruction and darkness is not as far-fetched as it sounds at first.

Imagine looking up into a full sun, but instead of it blistering your eyes with that red-light circle you can still see with your eyes shut, it just sort of blinks at you like a shorting-out light bulb. You go outside later that night, and the moon is no more than a fuzzy, vague smudge in the sky. The Big Dipper has no handle. The North Star has gone south.

Darkness. Even when you're surrounded by familiar things, the dark has the power to distort and disorient. But in a world that's growing scarier and less familiar by the hour—like the one described in these trumpet blasts—the horror of watching the sun fail, flicker, and come close to a full power outage is going to be terrifying indeed!

Verse 12. Why would God do this to the world He created? Hadn't He promised Noah that "day and night" would never cease "as long as the earth endures"? (Genesis 8:22). Yes, but what you're witnessing in Revelation 8 is the dismantling of the earth. At the time of the trumpet judgments, the earth is no longer "enduring." It's dying. Creation is crumbling. The truly amazing thing is that, even with the earth coming apart at the seams, with repentance and salvation still available to lost humanity, many will still choose to reject Him (see 9:20). Even with God's power on full display, some will still love "darkness rather than the light" (John 3:19).

8:13 Warning—It Gets Worse!

Perhaps you have a family friend who's in the final stages of cancer, and you know there's no hope for recovery outside of the direct, miraculous intervention of God. Who knows, then, how much more pain he or she will still have to go through? At this point, death would be a relief, but until it happens, the next days, weeks—whatever—are going to be nothing but bad and worse.

We are witnessing in the first four trumpet judgments a widespread, devastating blow to our planet. Yet in the midst of falling stars, beached whales, and wildfires, a lone eagle soars unshaken above the scenes of destruction. The earth, yes, is dying, and it's not going to get better. In fact, it's about to get even worse—*"woe, woe, woe"* worse! With the soon-to-come, withering blare of trumpets five, six, and seven, not only the earth but also its human inhabitants are in grave danger.

WOE.
This disaster-warning word foretells the cursed consequences of living in conflict with God's values, the unhappy results of clinging to ungodly decisions and lifestyles.

These trumpet judgments don't square with the theory of evolution, which says that species will continue to grow, adapt, and thrive. Do you still wonder if God created the heavens and the earth? Why?

_____

_____

_____

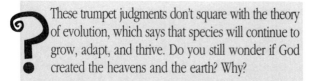

Revelation 9

9:1-6 Trumpet #5—The Abyss Opens Up

Have you ever been through a locust summer? If you have, you know what it's like when the bushes, brick walls, and fence posts are covered with crispy locust skins, when every treetop is screeching day and night with the squeals of their mating calls, when you can't take a simple walk to the car without ducking for low-flying, broad-winged, bug-eyed creepy crawlers. It's shiveringly scary.

But nothing like this.

ABYSS.

This is a bottomless pit [uh-BISS] that refers to either the place of the dead or [in this case] the home of the demonic. The demons known as "Legion," which Jesus drove from a possessed man, begged Him not to "banish them" there [Luke 8:31].

FIVE MONTHS.

Several of these temporary lengths of time——like this one in verse 5——appear in the book of Revelation. These are probably never to be taken literally. They simply denote that this trouble will last for a God-defined period of time, both to punish sin and attract repentance.

ABADDON.

This high-ranking demon [uh-BAD-un], also known as Apollyon [uh-POLLY-on], appears six times in the Old Testament as a synonym for sheol or the place of the dead. Look for references to him in Job, Psalms, and Proverbs. His name means "destruction."

Look Out for Locusts (verses 1-6)

We usually think of death as being our ultimate fear. But think about it this way: Can you imagine *wanting* to die but not being *able* to? Can you imagine being in so much pain that death would seem like a welcome relief . . . but death wouldn't come? The torture only continued?

That's the unhappy news of verse 5, where a band of stinging "locusts" are given this mission: not to eat tree leaves or to strip wheat fields (verse 4), but "to torment" those who don't have "God's seal on their foreheads" (remember this protective mark from 7:3). This is important: "to torment" them, but not "to kill" them.

So who's the one calling for this locust plague? God is. It seems surprising, doesn't it, that He's the One who has "the key" to the abyss (verse 1). But He's the One who's in total control, setting the strategy, and securing His people from danger.

Next question: Who are these scorpion-tailed hell-bugs going after? Not the children of God, who are declared off limits, but the unbelievers. That's right, these demonic "locusts" pour out of their dark, smoky shaft to irritate the irreligious.

You'd think, of course, that unbelievers wouldn't be targets of demons. You'd think no one could command Satan's warriors to go after the God-haters. After all, aren't they on the same side? But we'll see this again in Revelation, especially late in chapter 17: the Devil doesn't just hate God and His people. He even hates his own, who have the same evil desires as he does.

He's sickening, isn't he?

Face to Face with a Demon (verses 7-12)

Have you ever wondered what a demon looks like? We don't know for sure. And even though the language of this passage is probably more figurative than literal, this particular passage of Scripture is more descriptive of demons than any other in all the Bible. They're fallen angels, with no hope of redemption. They're ugly, noisy, and disgusting.

They have:

- men's faces with long, women's hair,
- sharp teeth and clanking, iron breastplates,
- ferocious, flapping wings and stinging tails.

Gross. We also get a look at their "king." This is most likely not Satan, who doesn't show his face until later . . . in chapter 12. Instead, this is probably some kind of arch-demon or head honcho who calls the shots in this rotten, rat-hole regiment.

The next time some temptation comes looking for you, seeming so sweet and harmless and not worth the fight of resisting, remember what the Devil's minions really look like. Will that help?

DEMON RANKS.
It's not abundantly clear from this passage, but it seems logical that—just as there are orders of angels in heaven—there is also rank and position in the demon realm. Some do one thing, some do another. Some are in command, others in submission.

9:13-21 Trumpet #6—Horse Stampede

Demons on Horseback (verses 13-19)

Don't be confused by the "four angels" in verses 14-15. Like some of the "angels" that parade around as nearly naked, arena football cheerleaders, these are not the valiant warrior messengers of God. Make no mistake: these are demons, angels in rebellion, otherworldly creatures who've gone over to the other side. With the blast of the sixth trumpet, these "angels" are released on the earth . . . to kill.

Now, try to get this picture in your mind: two hundred million horses. No, wait—not just horses, but fire-breathing dragon-horses with tails like snakes that bite and poison as they pass you. Oh, and also—each of these smoke-blowing beasts is topped by an armored rider who's looking for the first available human to gallop toward and trample underfoot.

GOD'S TIMETABLE.
You're going to come across a lot of people who don't think there's a God who's in control of time and eternity. But look at Him here in verse 15, snapping the four angels into position at the exact "hour, day, month, and year" He had prescribed before time began.

EUPHRATES.
This ancient river [yoo-FRAY-teez], specifically mentioned in the garden of Eden, flows to the east of Israel. The Parthians, an Iranian people who lived across this river in John's day, bore some of the characteristics and battle tactics of the wretched warriors in this passage. Some interpret this to mean that a literal army will attack from the East, but these monsters seem more demonic than human.

REPENT?

Even with God's power on full display, some will still love "darkness rather than the light" (John 3:19). Some will continue to accept death when they could easily have life. Some will "not repent" (verse 21) no matter what we say or what we do.

WITNESSING.

The sad fact that many people will not repent of their sins—no matter what—should never make us shy about sharing Christ's love with others. In fact, it should encourage us with the knowledge that we're not responsible for how they respond, but we must be willing to tell them.

DEMONS.

One other unusual thing about demons is that, while they can sin, they cannot repent. Redemption is something they can't understand.

Did you know this kind of movie-screen spectacle was in the Bible? You're reading it for yourself—except here, the plot's not cool and the suffering's not over in two hours. For those who'd rather face a sulfur-spitting monster who's trying to kill them than submit to the suffering Savior who died for them, the prognosis is bad and the future is scary. In the trumpet scene just before this—the locust swarm—the plan was to torture but not to kill. This time, however, death is in the offing.

Still Not Convinced (verses 20-21)

It's amazing how deeply the Devil can deceive us. We can know beyond the shadow of a doubt that going to a particular party is going to cause us temptation trouble, but we just might go anyway. That's because the Devil is a trick artist, an illusionist, a slick-talking cold-heart.

Want proof? He can convince a person who's just watched a horde of hell horses come *this close* to bashing his head in, that "worshiping demons" is still a good idea (verse 20). Man! You'd think every one of these people would fling themselves headlong on God's mercy seat, begging for shelter and a chance to escape. Something inside them, though, tells them they're right where they ought to be. Incredible!

God loves people so much, however, that He's willing to give them this painful preview of what *every day* will be like for them throughout eternity if they don't repent and turn from their "murders, their sorceries, their sexual immorality, or their thefts" (verse 21). Surely they'll see what tortures await them.

Won't they?

Revelation 10

Again—just like with the seals at the start of chapter 7—just when you thought the sixth trumpet would be immediately followed by the seventh, there's a break in the action. This time, we'll have to wait nearly two chapters (all the way to 11:15) before the final trumpet blows. But it won't be a boring, stand-still interlude. We've got some serious action coming up.

10:1-7 Don't Repeat This

Not too long ago we got a peek at the big old "angel of the abyss" (9:11). Remember how creepy he and his buddies looked? Compare him now to the "mighty angel coming down from heaven" (verse 1)—the rainbow around him, the sun in his face, the glowing strength of his legs, the voice (instead of teeth) like a lion. Whose side would you rather be on?

Here's another question: How good are you at keeping a secret? I guess when "a voice from heaven" warns you not to tell it to anybody, you have a little more incentive to keep from spilling. But on the other hand, if it's a secret so big that it takes "seven thunders" to explain it to you (verse 4), it must be something pretty spectacular, pretty hard to keep to yourself.

So here in this electric moment, with a towering angel straddling the last remaining remnants of a dying earth, with the seventh trumpet held back for an "interval of time" (verse 6), we wait with John, unable to speak, amazed at God's "hidden plan" unfolding before our eyes.

SEVEN THUNDERS.
Of all the characters in the book of Revelation, these are perhaps the most mysterious. Except for assuming they're big and loud and full of heavenly authority, nobody really knows what these "thunders" are.

UNSPEAKABLE.
The Apostle Paul related an experience in 2 Corinthians 12:1-4 when he also had some kind of glorious revelation. He, too, was either forbidden to tell about it or had no human words to describe it.

ANGELS AND SCROLLS.
Several Old Testament prophets had an experience similar to John's. Ezekiel, in particular, testified to seeing an angel surrounded by light, clouds, and a rainbow (Ezekiel 1:26-28). He also was given a scroll to eat (Ezekiel 2:8—3:3) that was "sweet as honey" to his taste, though bitter with words of "lamentation, mourning, and woe."

Verse 4. If the report of the "seven thunders" has anything to do with the imminent outpouring of God's judgment, why would John not be permitted to tell it? If this heaven-sent insight could be the difference between someone turning from their sins or tumbling into hell, why keep it quiet? The truth is, everything that anyone needs to know about their own sinful condition and God's offer of forgiveness is already obvious enough. Yes, the details about how the earth will end are worth our study, but knowing all about it is not necessary for salvation. We need God, and He has come to us in Jesus—that's already well-known. It's all anyone needs to know.

UNIVERSALISM.
Some people believe that everyone is going to heaven, no matter what. This is called universalism—which would be kind of "sweet" to believe. God Himself, in fact, says He doesn't "take any pleasure in the death of the wicked" (Ezekiel 18:23). But that doesn't keep people from rejecting Him every day and sealing their own doom by their disbelief. His salvation must be received (1 John 5:12). Just because something's "bitter" doesn't make it untrue.

LITTLE SCROLL.
This is not the same "scroll" as the earlier one with the seven seals (5:1). This scroll "lies open in the hand of the angel" (verse 8) and contains the completion of God's plan for final judgment and redemption.

10:8-11 The Bittersweet Scroll

There will come a time in your life—if it hasn't come already—when a foot-long cheese chili dog won't just cost you two dollars and a half, but also enough heartburn to keep you awake half the night. Sometimes things that feel good going down don't stay that way after you've eaten them.

John's experience with the "little scroll" (verse 9) was sort of similar to this. It's true that God's Word is "sweet as honey" in many ways. It encourages us, it inspires us, it reminds us of God's deep love and His never-ending reliability.

But being obedient to the Scriptures is indeed a high-cost proposition. There is a bitter side to it. We have many friends, for example, who are gambling they'll never have to deal with the God of the Bible. It hurts us to think that they might never change, that they might end up in hell forever. The Bible is indeed a truthful mix of amazingly good news and frighteningly bad news.

We sometimes like to think that Christianity is all fuzz and fluff, but it's truly as heavy as it is heavenly. That's why we need to be as courageous as John was—willing to proclaim the truth of God's Word even when it hurts, even when it runs the risk of offending, even when it costs us.

Have you ever had to play the role of prophet, telling someone what God's Word says about something, even if it wasn't easy to talk about?

_____

_____

_____

SWEET AS HONEY.
The Bible uses this language several times (Psalm 119:103) to describe the way believers feel about the words of Scripture (Jeremiah 15:16).

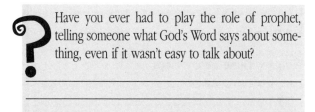

Revelation 11

We're still waiting for the seventh trumpet to sound, and—here at the halfway point of the book—we're inching into the part of Revelation that's most mysterious and hard to understand. So hang tight! We won't answer all your questions, but at least we'll all know a little more than we did before.

MEASURING ROD.
For two Old Testament parallels that are amazing in their similarity to verses 1-2—much more descriptive even, go to Ezekiel 40—42 as well as Zechariah 2.

11:1-6 The Two Witnesses

Measuring the Temple (verses 1-2)

Sometimes, one of the best ways to handle Revelation is to look for overarching themes rather than haggling over unknowable details. That's why, when you come to a passage like this—the one about measuring "God's sanctuary and the altar"—perhaps it's best to settle for the big picture without insisting on a close-up.

The theme that comes through most clearly in this first section of the chapter is God's protection of His people. Yes, the Bible tells us to expect hardship, persecution, and (for many) death at the hands of cruel Christian haters. But remember this: God has numbered His people (verse 1).

HOLY CITY.
Hard to tell whether this is actually Jerusalem or is more symbolic of the church as a whole; but whatever it is, "the nations" are permitted to "trample" on it for "42 months." This is commonly considered the first half of the seven-year tribulation.

He knows who we are. We are ultimately and eternally safe in His hands.

TWO WITNESSES.
In biblical thinking, the rules were: "A fact must be established by the testimony of two or three witnesses" [Deuteronomy 19:15]. These "two witnesses" appearing together in Revelation 11, then, are the Bible's way of verifying the absolute truth of their message.

OLIVE TREES.
The fruit of these trees provides the oil that lights the lampstands. This olive oil is symbolic of the power of the Holy Spirit—"'not by strength or by might, but by My Spirit,' says the Lord" [Zechariah 4:6].

Who Are These Two? (verses 3-6)

Have you ever done any door-to-door evangelism, maybe around your church or during a mission trip? How did it go? How difficult was it? How were you received? If you have some firsthand answers to questions like these, then you can identify in a small way with the ministry of the "two witnesses" (verse 3). There's something about being a witness that can make your knees knock together sometimes.

These "two witnesses," though—who are they? Some interpret them as being two historical figures (like Moses and Elijah), or the combined "witnesses" of the Old and New Testaments (the Law and the Gospel), or perhaps two unknown people who will emerge as Christian leaders in the future.

One of the more intriguing guesses says that the "two witnesses" are not two individuals but the end-time church as a whole. One reason for thinking this is because they're described as being "lampstands," which corresponds with the specific analogy Jesus made in 1:20.

Whoever they are, look at the power these witnesses have! (verses 5-6). As the final days heat up, the intensity of the battle—as well as the evaporation of any religious middle ground—will inspire these two to live up to their privilege, empowered by the Spirit to stand boldly for Him and display His holy strength.

Why does it so often take a state of emergency like this before we (like the two witnesses) are able to put all our eggs in Christ's basket, to pray for His help and exercise His power?

11:7-10 A Premature Funeral

Think of some of the classic movies you loved when you were a kid. Or think about some of the films you might have seen lately, where the story's turning point happened at almost the last minute. In every one of these—and dozens more—just when you thought all was lost and the main characters were done for, help arrived at the last minute.

This passage is one of those scenes, when just before the end things look utterly hopeless. After "1,260 days" of intense conflict, the enemy pulls out the big bomb, the secret weapon, the "beast" from the "abyss"—the antichrist. The witnesses are overpowered, murdered, their bodies left to rot in the city streets like in some grainy video clip from a dusty, war-torn country.

You've seen stuff like this on television—people leaping up and down, smiling for the cameras, celebrating with raised flags and grisly souvenirs from the scene. Shouting victory slogans and dancing in the streets, the conquerors appear practically drunk on the violence. This is just like the people in this passage who are gloating and throwing parties, delighted that the depressing, doomsday voices of the witnesses have finally been silenced (they think) for good. This gift-giving, big bash atmosphere (verse 10) reveals how deep the unbelievers' hatred for God will become.

THE ANTICHRIST.
You'll read a lot more about this "beast" in chapter 13, but for now let's just say he's the evil leader who will raise himself up near the end of time, claiming to be Christ, leading the world in opposition of Christ, but actually being everything Christ is not.

SYMBOLICALLY SPEAKING.
John makes it clear in verse 8 that he is speaking "prophetically," using terms that are meant to be taken as word pictures, not as literal reports. The "three and a half days," for example—half of the perfect number seven—are thought by some to represent, not half a week, but a distinct period of time equal to half of the tribulation period. To see this in Old Testament prophecy, explore your way through Daniel 9:24-27.

SODOM AND EGYPT.
The ancient city of Sodom (SOD-um) was renowned for its extreme wickedness (Genesis 18:20). Egypt, of course, was the nation that enslaved God's people for hundreds of years until the Exodus. Together, these cities represent sin and evil.

TAKEN TO HEAVEN.
This is reminiscent of what happened to the Old Testament characters Enoch (Genesis 5:24) and Elijah (2 Kings 2:11).

FIRST, SECOND, THIRD WOE.
The first woe (or expression of God's wrath and judgment) was the locust attack of the fifth trumpet (9:12). The second woe was apparently the sixth trumpet—the 200 million horsemen. Now that this one-and-one-half-chapter interlude is over, the "third woe"—the end of the world—is set to take place.

11:11-14 Not So Fast

What a turn of events! For some unknown period of time ("three and a half days" in Revelation talk), the bodies of the slain witnesses have been decomposing in broad daylight, much to the delight of those who relished their defeat.

But suddenly, the dead are on their feet—alive! A "loud voice from heaven" is calling them home from their temporary place of torture and humiliation. Then, as a final exclamation point, the earth begins to tremble and quake, killing the killers by the thousands and sending the "survivors" to their knees, keenly aware of God's power.

11:15-19 Trumpet #7—Heavy Weather and Heavenly Worship

Finally, above the rumble of earthquakes, the shrieks of the dying, and the blubbering prayers of the stunned survivors, the last trumpet peals out loud, crisp, and strong. The redeemed who have already died—believers in Christ who are now in heaven, free from the end-time terrors of the earth—burst forth in worshipful song. Maybe you've heard a version of this line in the "Hallelujah Chorus" from Handel's Messiah: "The kingdom of the world has become the kingdom of our Lord and of His Messiah, and He will reign forever and ever!" (verse 15).

So this is the end of the trumpet series that began back in chapter 8. And just like the "seventh seal" of the scroll (8:1), which opened to reveal the "seven trumpets" (8:2), the blast of this final trumpet is not so much a happening as it is another revelation. This time, the curtain is pulled back on the "bowl" judgments, which will show up a little later (chapters 15–16).

In the meantime, though—as always in Revelation—it's a good time to worship (verses 16-18). The "24 elders" lead the way (remember them from 4:4 and 5:8), praising God for His . . .

- Unchangeableness—"the Almighty, who is and who was" and will always be the same
- Reigning power—His complete dominance over every so-called rival and challenger
- Justice—His holy judgment against sin and those who harm others with it
- Willingness to reward—His desire to give rest to those who have served Him
- Impartiality—His love for both "small and great," people of all ages and nationalities
- Sovereignty—His full control over all things, His power to keep His promises

Lightning streaks across the sky, and thunder rumbles in response. The ground shimmies and shakes, and pelting hail carves grooves in a dying earth. God's eternal reign begins to be established, and we get set for one final look back (chapter 12) at the grand history of spiritual conflict.

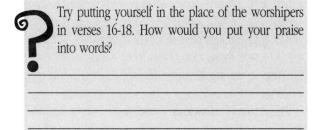

Try putting yourself in the place of the worshipers in verses 16-18. How would you put your praise into words?

_____

_____

_____

_____

SANCTUARY.
Whether symbolic or actual, the incredible sight of verse 19—God's temple or sanctuary (meaning "holy place") being revealed in all its heavenly glory—is among the most breathtaking scenes in all of Revelation. The last temple in Israel had been destroyed in A.D. 70, nearly thirty years before. For John—a faithful, lifelong Jew—seeing it again must have melted his heart in worship, relief, and wonder.

ARK OF THE COVENANT.
This was the original container for the Ten Commandments that sat in the holiest part of the tabernacle (later, the temple) and represented the presence of God to the people (1 Kings 8:6). It was lost to history six centuries before Christ when the Babylonians took Israel captive. This vision of it (verse 19) reveals its eternal, heavenly counterpart.

Revelation 12

THE WOMAN.
In Roman Catholic thought, the woman in this passage is Mary, the mother of Christ. It's easy to see why you could think that. But especially as you keep reading the rest of the chapter, you'll sense that this woman is way more than one person. She represents all of God's people—first the nation of Israel (from whom the Son was born) and later the church, "persecuted" by the enemy (verse 13) yet protected by God's love and power (verse 16).

DIADEMS.
These (DIE-uh-dims) are crowns or head coverings of some kind that symbolize authority and honor.

INFANT DEATH.
This makes you think of the story from Matthew 2:16-18, when King Herod massacred all the boys "who were two years old and under" around Bethlehem in an attempt to kill Jesus.

For the next few chapters, (at least through chapter 14), imagine you're sitting in a theatre for a play performance. This is not just any play, but one that advertises itself as a composite view of all human history—past, present, and future—sort of like those year-in-review things they show on TV around the end of December.

Remember, too, that this chapter doesn't follow chronologically after chapter 11. This is another interlude or intermission of sorts. So sit back and . . . get ready.

12:1-6 History Lesson

When the curtain opens on this play, you see a pregnant woman already in labor. As if this wasn't intense enough, a "fiery red dragon"—Satan—storms onto the scene, sending fear into the heart of the woman by showing off his star power. If he can just "devour her child" (verse 4)—if he can just put a stop to the birth of this "Son" who has the power Satan so wants for himself—this is his only chance (he thinks).

This "dragon" is vicious, bloodthirsty, potent. Imagine the pent-up power it takes to sweep away "a third of the stars in heaven" and hurl them down to earth (verse 4). Wow!

But his threats are just talk. Although he's standing right "in front" of the woman who's "about to give birth" (verse 4), he can't touch the child before he's "caught up to God and to His throne" (verse 5). The Son is safe. But the woman is not—or at least she doesn't feel like it. So she runs into the wilderness in dread of the dragon's fury, in search of God's protection.

12:7-13 A Battle in Heaven

Satan Thrown to Earth (verses 7-9)

When the curtain rises again, the scene is set in heaven—the site of a cosmic battle between warring angels. Imagine what this is like!—supernatural armies pummeling each other with wonder-world weaponry. Try as he might, though, Satan and his forces can't do anything to avoid being booted out of heaven.

Verses 7-8. It seems so weird that Satan somehow has (or has had) access to heaven. How could that be? Remember that he was once an angel, but he rebelled against God. He fell (like all fallen angels) beyond the ability to repent. Yet God in His sovereignty gives him the ability to temporarily horn in on heavenly affairs (see Job 1:6-12). This is why, according to chapter 21, God will one day create a "new heaven," one that's not stained by Satan's footprints and battle scars. How wonderful it will be when God chooses to no longer grant him access to His ear.

Heaven Rejoices (verses 10-13)

How have you sensed Satan accusing you? One way he does it is by discouraging us with past failures, making it seem like a waste of time for us to get up and try again. Another way he accuses us is by questioning our sincerity, or even making us accuse other people.

It really doesn't matter, though, because he has no power over us—only the power we choose to give him. Why? How?

- "The blood of the Lamb"—Jesus defeated Satan on the cross, forgiving us of our sins and conquering the power of death and the Devil.
- "The word of [our] testimony"—our ongoing obedience and belief in Christ keeps Satan in his place.

Add to this a life of fearless confidence in God's ultimate power and victory—not loving our lives on earth so much,

ABORTION.
You can't come away from this passage without seeing who's behind our culture's rush toward killing the unborn. Certainly, abortion is more than a political issue. It's a highly personal situation involving crisis and tragedy on all sides. But death is Satan's stock-in-trade all throughout Revelation. He loves "to kill and to destroy," unlike Jesus, who came that we might "have life" (John 10:10).

MICHAEL.
He is an archangel (ARK-angel)—one of the highest ranking of them all—who is seen in Daniel 10:10-21; 12:1, guarding and defending the nation of Israel.

SATAN'S FALL.
We don't know a lot about this mysterious occurrence, but the best picture we get of it (besides verses 7-9) comes from Isaiah 14:12-20, of a "morning star" being flung to the earth, apparently before the creation of man. Also check out Jesus' statement in Luke 10:18. Whether verses 7-9 indicate that this still has a future-tense aspect to it is unclear.

DUALISM.
Some people believe that good and evil are equal forces in the universe, constantly duking it out to see which one will win (dual meaning "two"—dualism). The Star Wars movies are pretty much based on this theology. But the outcome of the battle in verses 7-9 is never in doubt. God and Satan are not head-to-head rivals. The only authority Satan has is the power that God has allowed him to have. There's no question that God is in ultimate control here.

EAGLES AND SERPENTS.
The swift, sturdy swoop of the "eagle" is a biblical picture of God's power and protection (Exodus 19:4). The "serpent" is a throwback to the first appearance of Satan in the Bible (Genesis 3:1-7). He's been sneaking around here ever since.

WATER MIRACLE.
This won't be the first time God has forced a body of water to break from its normal course and bend to His will. Remember the parting of the Red Sea (Exodus 14) and the crossing of the Jordan River (Joshua 3).

not forgetting how much better it's going to be in heaven. When we do this consistently, we can spend a lot more time rejoicing (verse 12) and a lot less time repenting!

The Devil is nothing but a liar who "knows he has a short time." He comprehends that God has a leash around his neck. So let Satan threaten and "accuse" us all he wants to (verse 10). Our King Jesus is here with "salvation" and "power" and "authority" in His hands—not for a "short time" but for all time.

> How has Satan used his primary tactic of deception to trick and trip you up? How has he been deceptive in your family's life? In your friends' lives?
>
> _____
> _____
> _____
> _____
> _____

12:13-18 Battle Aftermath

You can be staring out a window, imagining what a new car would look like in your driveway, and still—in the very same window—you can also spot the reflection of your little brother sneaking up from behind to scare you.

The drama of chapter 12 has this same kind of double-exposure property. It talks about things that are still to come, yet in the same breath, it talks about things that are happening right now or have already been.

For example, we know that the "dragon" (the Devil) has been persecuting the "woman" (ancient Israel, the church, God's people across time) for as long as history has been recorded. Past tense. Present tense. But it's very likely that in the final days—future tense—he'll crank up the heat to a maximum setting.

Whatever Satan tries to do, though, God has still promised to provide us a "place in the wilderness" (verse 14), the assurance of basic shelter and daily bread, even the awesome option of supernatural deliverance (verse 16).

Again, this doesn't mean persecution won't hurt. It doesn't mean it won't affect our lifestyle. It doesn't even mean that all of us will come out of the tribulation alive! But no matter how furiously Satan snarls at the end-time generation of believers (verse 17), he cannot ultimately win. He can "wage war," but he cannot prevail.

TIME, TIMES, HALF A TIME.
This unusual description first shows up in Daniel 7:25. If you insert the word "year" for the word "time" and then do some simple math, you can figure that the first "time" is one year, "times" equals two years, and "half a time" is six months—all of which adds up to three and one half years—half of the seven-year tribulation period.

Revelation 13

13:1-4 The Antichrist

The antichrist is coming one day. He may not be born yet, but he might. He could be 12 or 15 or 25 or 48. We don't know what he'll look like, who his parents were or will be, whether he'll grow up in church, in poverty, or on the upper-class track to success.

All we know is that when the curtain fell on chapter 12, Satan looked totally thwarted and defeated. With his tail between his legs, he went to the seashore—his own little beach hideaway—to ponder what to do next. Plan B.

And here it is: Antichrist. The opposite of Christ. The one who is everything Christ is not. The one who is against everything Christ is and stands for.

He is Satan's puppet on a string, a parody of the living Christ. Is he monstrously ugly? You wouldn't think so, not the way people are flocking to him and worshiping him (verse 4). But he is powerful—and it shows—from his

TEN HORNS.
As mentioned earlier, "horns" in prophetic literature don't refer to pointy protrusions from the top of the head, but are rather a symbol of actual power (Psalm 18:2). Having "ten horns" simply means that the power of this beast is great.

BLASPHEMY.
This [BLASS-fum-ee] is the deliberate act of publicly mocking God's deity, showing outright disrespect for His name and character, calling those things that are evil good, while calling good those things that are evil. In the antichrist's case, it also means the act of claiming to be God or God-like.

LEOPARD, BEAR, LION.
These same descriptions appear in Daniel 7:1-6, which (in Daniel's dream) represented three hostile empires—Babylon, Greece, and Rome—the last two definitely coming from the Mediterranean Sea side of Israel. (The antichrist comes "up out of the sea," remember?) Just who will fill in the blank as the final agent of world domination? We don't know yet.

imposing presence to his bragging rights, from his head to his feet (verses 1-2). He even has some kind of self-healing power. He will be able to come back from a killing blow to the head—a "fatal wound"—which is either symbolic of the defeat of his cause at the cross or something that has happened physically to this particular person.

Verse 4. The antichrist—who is he? When will he appear? How will we know him? It certainly appears that it will be a person, an extraordinarily wicked and persuasive human being "who opposes and exalts himself above every so-called god or object of worship, so that he sits in God's sanctuary, publicizing that he himself is God" (2 Thessalonians 2:4). Some people believe that it's more than one person—perhaps an empire-building nation or coalition (Nazi Germany comes to mind as an example), intent on evil, domination, and destruction. Perhaps this is true, but rarely does this occur without one person being the face of the entire nation or movement.

42 MONTHS.
Once again, this number (equal to the "1,260 days" mentioned in 11:3) squares with the three and one half years we've been seeing as a repeating element in the tribulation timetable.

BOOK OF LIFE.
This is God's own listing of the saved and redeemed, whose names have only been placed there by their faith and trust in "the Lamb who was slaughtered" (verse 8).

13:5-10 A Beastly Reign

We've heard about nations where dictators rule by torture, threat, and discrimination. We've seen pictures in our history books of bloody wars between nations, of bodies piled up in mass graves. We've read about the cruel atrocities people are capable of performing when under the deception of a maniacal ruler.

But we haven't seen anything yet. The "42-month" reign of the antichrist is going to be more deadly, more merciless, and more widespread than anything our world has ever seen. It's going to be totally godless, a direct hit against believers of "every tribe, people, language, and nation" (verse 7).

This antichrist is going to have power "given to him"—by God Himself!—to blaspheme God (verse 5). He is going to be a picture of pride at its fullest. That's because human arrogance always leads to blasphemy. It is pride and arrogance that enables us to sit in front of a TV sitcom that defaces our God and everything He loves and stands for. It is self-love that allows us to be entertained by untruth.

All those who take part in this end-times onslaught—all of them—all those who are fully in favor of crushing the Christians—will "worship" this beastly antichrist, doing anything he says, hanging on his every word, and thinking this is finally the last gasp of the God of the Bible.

Well, we'll see about that, won't we? This great hope is what fuels "the endurance and the faith of the saints."

Verse 7. Perhaps you thought God was going to be protecting His people, not handing them over for slaughter. Well, if we were to tell you that by shoving somebody to the ground, we were "protecting" them from being hit by a car, you'd say, "Thanks for pushing me!" Right? The big picture (the possibility of being run over) puts the smaller picture (a shove in the back) in context. God never promised we wouldn't suffer for our faith. To use our traffic analogy, He never said we wouldn't be shoved around a little. But He did say we would "never be harmed by the second death" (2:11). We will finally and ultimately be safe—"protected"—in His arms.

How different would your life look if you saw yourself from an eternal perspective? What would matter more to you? What would matter less?

_____

_____

_____

_____

DESTINY.

One of the hardest Bible concepts to understand is the contrast of free will versus predestination—the idea that our destinies are predetermined by God. The plain truth from verses 8-10 is that the names of all believers were known "from the foundation of the world." Those who were "destined for captivity" find themselves held captive in the end. The amazing thing, though, is that God maintains this kind of complete knowledge while still allowing each person the freedom of choice. He alone is able to handle such power and remain lovingly and perfectly fair about it. Yes, our days are planned, yet we are not robotically controlled. We can look on this, then, as freedom, not confinement—a reason to trust, not to feel trapped.

13:11-18 The False Prophet

The Beast from the Earth (verses 11-15)

Have you ever been taken in by a phony? Have you ever bought something that was supposed to do this or that for you but ended up doing nothing—or perhaps even made things worse? Have you ever felt really close to someone who was so persuasive, so compelling, but who turned out to be a big fake and a fraud?

Meet the "beast coming up out of the earth"—the end-times worship leader. He is the third evil being on the scene. Working in tandem with the antichrist, this show-boating cheerleader is going to have a real dragon-like side to go along with his lamb-like appearance (verse 11). For example:

- "He performs great signs"—cool carnival tricks like making fireballs flash out of the sky.
- "He deceives" people into thinking that worshiping the antichrist is the wave of the future.
- He even gives the image of this beast the ability to "speak"—AND to reach out and kill anyone who doesn't bow down in its presence.

The Mark of the Beast (verses 16-18)

Imagine if someone you knew well—a pretty close friend—believed in this false prophet. Imagine what it would be like to see her or him wearing the "666" tattoo, the "name of the beast," (verse 18), the trademark of the evil one.

This season of whacked-out, false religious fervor will spell the end of the age of tolerance. Only those who have his "mark" on their "right hand" or "forehead" (verse 16) will be able to buy things at the grocery store or perform business of any kind. It'll be his way or the highway.

Hmm. People always said Christians were so arrogant for claiming that there was only one true way. Well, these guys sure don't mind claiming one way for themselves, do they? For now, anyway.

This is such a serious place of conflict and contrast in the book of Revelation. On the one hand, we see the antichrist and the false prophet tagging cocky yet cowardly unbelievers with a 666 mark of devilish doom. While on the other hand, we read about the Lamb's "book of life," a holy listing of the saved and secure. No matter how you slice it, life always comes down to this.

So maybe it's a good time to stop and make it really clear what God's salvation is all about.

Here's the History

The Bible says that all around us—in the predictability of the sunrise, in the return of springtime, in the papery precision of a wasp's nest, in a thousand million ways—we see the idea that God is living, active, and real, "being understood through what He has made." This is called general revelation—the fact that God's "eternal power and divine nature" have been made known to everyone. "As a result, people are without excuse" (Romans 1:20).

But in Jesus, God has made himself fully known. "He is the image of the invisible God" (Colossians 1:15). "He is the radiance of His glory, the exact expression of His nature, and He sustains all things by His powerful word" (Hebrews 1:3). Every promise made to us by God has been fulfilled in Jesus Christ. This special revelation we have received by getting to see, hear, and know the Son of God brings us face-to-face with Him—as well as with ourselves.

Here's the Deal

(1) *In light of His perfection, we find ourselves to be sinners*—"Guilty" even before we were born; already "sinful" when our mothers conceived us (Psalm 51:5). "There is no one righteous, not even one" (Romans 3:10). "All have sinned and fall short of the glory of God" (Romans 3:23).

(2) *In light of His coming to earth, we find ourselves loved*—For when the time was just right, "God sent His Son, born of a woman, born under the law, to redeem those under the law, so that we might receive adoption as sons" (Galatians 4:4-5). "We love because He first loved us" (1 John 4:19).

(3) *In light of such grace, we find ourselves needing to repent and believe*—"'The message is near you, in your mouth and in your heart.' ... If you confess with your mouth, 'Jesus is Lord,' and believe in your heart that God raised Him from the dead, you will be saved" (Romans 10:8-9).

(4) *In light of His death—if we believe in Him—we will find ourselves forgiven*— "For rarely will someone die for a just person . . . but God proves His own love for us in that while we were still sinners Christ died for us" (Romans 5:7-8). "He has rescued us from the domain of darkness" and forgiven our sins (Colossians 1:13-14).

(5) *In light of His resurrection—again, if we believe in Him—we can find ourselves unafraid*—For He has "abolished death and has brought life and immortality to light" (2 Timothy 1:10). "O Death, where is your victory? O Death, where is your sting?" We now have "victory through our Lord Jesus Christ" (1 Corinthians 15:55-57).

Jesus has done it all—lived a perfect life, died in our place, defeated death, and won for us an eternity with Him in heaven. The One who made us has come to save us . . . because He loves us.

What Do You Say?

If you're just now coming around to believing this for the first time, if you're ready to admit your need and to turn away from your sins—to turn toward a life that's way better than anything this world has to offer—then pray this prayer right now:

Lord God,

You have shown me today that I have no hope without You. I can't keep from sinning and messing up. It's part of who I am. So I give up trying to make myself a better person. Instead, I need You to make me a new person. I confess my sins. I believe in You—in Your life, in Your death, in Your return from the grave. I am ready to receive the salvation You have promised—a life of peace and joy on earth, a life of unending love with You forever. Come into my heart, Lord Jesus. I need You—now!

Revelation 14

14:1-5 The Lamb and the 144,000

Singing a New Song (verses 1-3)

Maybe you're a songwriter. Perhaps you like to write poetry or just your own thoughts in a journal. If you do, have you ever been dying to write something fresh and new, but nothing came to mind? You just stared at that blank, empty page, and waited . . . and waited . . . wadding up your weak, measly attempts, wishing something good would come to you. Frustrating, isn't it?

But think about how it feels when the words do start to flow, when the lyrics and the tune finally do come together. Whether anyone else ever hears it or not, it really doesn't matter, because you and God have a "new song" to sing. It's yours. Nobody else's.

That's a good feeling.

One day, those believers in Christ who've had to face the fire of tribulation are going to find themselves at home with the Lord, "redeemed from the earth" (verse 3). Beyond the reach of the antichrist and the false prophet, they'll gather together around the throne of God to celebrate the safety God has given them.

And they'll sing.

A Picture of Purity (verses 4-5)

Take a good look at the people gathered around the throne in this passage.

- They are "not defiled with women."
- They have "kept their virginity."

Here chastity is used as a symbol of moral purity and unswerving loyalty to Christ. In prophetic literature apostasy and rebellion are often described as adultery. Sure, Satan had tried before to teach them another song, but he couldn't make them learn it. Oh, it was tempting. It sounded nice at first. But somewhere in the distance, they kept

MOUNT ZION.
This originally referred to the fortified hill of Jerusalem. It later came to be synonymous with the temple, the capital city of Israel, or the city of God, the heavenly Jerusalem.

GOD'S NAME.
It's interesting that God's people have a distinguishing symbol that trumps the depressing "mark" of the beast. This "name" written on the believer's foreheads in heaven is God's "glorious and awesome name" (Deuteronomy 28:58), "the name that is above every name" (Philippians 2:9).

SEXUAL PURITY.
Several big sections of Proverbs 5—7 talk about the hazards of sexual promiscuity and the rewards of holy living. Also check out Job's self-proclaimed "covenant" with his eyes not to look lustfully at a woman (Job 31:1).

FIRSTFRUITS.
According to the Old Testament law, Israelites were to bring a portion of their first harvest—the best of the best—to present to God as an offering of gratitude (Numbers 15:17-21). This term is used in many later Bible passages to describe what God's people are like in His eyes—the most valuable of all His creation.

hearing this other song—the song of the Lamb.

• "No lie" is found "in their mouths."

• They are "blameless."

Yes, they were born with the depravity of man. They had every opportunity to buy into sin. But they didn't. They wouldn't. They remind us that it *can be done*—righteousness *can be lived*. Even when everything around us reeks of compromise and hypocrisy, when even our Christian brothers and sisters are able to lie so easily, when we're almost certain that everyone is doing it, God can still give us the power to say no and stand tall. They were "imitators of God" (Ephesians 5:1). Their character shown out in the midst of deepest darkness.

Ours can, too.

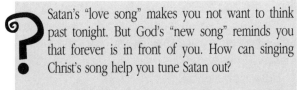

Satan's "love song" makes you not want to think past tonight. But God's "new song" reminds you that forever is in front of you. How can singing Christ's song help you tune Satan out?

_____

_____

_____

14:6-12 Three Angels' Announcements

BABYLON.
This was one of the earliest cities in civilization (Genesis 10:10—remember the "tower of Babel" in Genesis 11?). It became a symbol of man's pride and one of the major enemies of Israel, even taking the Jews captive and destroying their temple during Nebuchadnezzar's reign (2 Chronicles 36:5-7).

Your parents might warn you that if you don't get home by 11:30 tonight, you're grounded for the next two weeks. They're giving you a warning of what *might* happen. But sometimes warnings are more like *announcements*—warnings about outcomes you can't avoid. When these kinds of warnings come down, you're busted, caught red-handed. You know judgment day is coming and is absolutely certain.

This passage comes with *those* kinds of warnings—from three different messenger angels:

• *Angel #1.* Verse 6 says he comes with the "eternal gospel," which means "good news." But it's only good news for those who have put their faith in Christ, "because the hour of His judgment has come." And there's no getting around it from any point on the earth.

• *Angel #2.* We'll read a lot more about this wicked place called "Babylon" in the detailed visions of chapters 17 and 18, where this city's collapse is telescoped out into all kinds of horrors and colors. For now, let's leave it at this: the full payment on sin and unbelief is about to come due.

• *Angel #3.* During the time of the great tribulation, the world will pin all its hopes on the antichrist. They'll take a lot of stock in having his mark on their foreheads. They'll feel like they're in the club. But their rejection of Christ will get them a lot more than they bargained for—"the wine of God's wrath . . . mixed full strength in the cup of His anger" (verse 10).

These are warnings to the unsaved—a final call to repent and believe. Without a change of heart, unbelievers are faced with the "smoke" of "torment" that goes up "forever and ever" (verse 11). But these announcements are also meant to encourage the faithful to stand their ground, to endure, not to give up . . . because a day is coming when they can "rest from their labors" (verse 13). This day, too, is guaranteed to happen.

Verse 13. "Blessed are the dead"? That sounds like an odd way to put it. But just as we are given grace to live, just as God grants us the blessing of being in families and enjoying the good things of earthly life (like strawberry ice cream, wood-burning fireplaces, and graduation day), He also gives us—when the time is right—the grace to die. Especially for those living in the heat of tribulation, death will not be the great enemy it seems like to us today. Instead, it will be a welcome relief from their suffering, the opportunity to see their wrongs avenged and their God exalted. "Blessed are the dead"? Yeah . . . when you look at it that way.

GOD'S VERSUS SATAN'S WRATH.
Some people have a hard time dealing with the wrath (or anger) of God. They see it as being altogether un-God-like. But His holy wrath is different from Satan's self-absorbed and hateful anger (or man's, for that matter). Satan is liable to turn his terror on anyone for his own wicked reasons, while God's wrath is always a divine response to human sin and injustice.

SULFUR.
Better known in biblical terms by its combustible form (brimstone) —and always a chosen material of judgment—this mineral found in large quantities in Bible lands was known to burst into flame when earthquakes released hot gases from the earth's interior.

WHEAT HARVEST.
One of Jesus' most well-known parables centered around the wheat harvest. It's found in Matthew 13:24-30 and is carefully explained a little later in verses 36-43.

SICKLE.
This instrument had a curved blade of flint or metal used to cut stalks of grain, whose short handle usually required the user to bend near the ground while harvesting. It's among the oldest tools known to man, dating back thousands of years before Christ.

WINEPRESS.
In Bible days, grapes were squeezed by stamping on them with your feet, as the juice oozed into collection pits where it would ferment before being placed into wineskins.

14:14-20 The Wheat and the Winepress

Often in life, we're able to say fairly accurately that there are two types of people: Boys and girls, for one easy example. Givers and takers. Haves and have-nots. Dog people and cat people. It's amazing how many different ways this seems to work.

In the end, though, Jesus puts this one-or-the-other reality into two distinct categories: wheat-harvest people and grape-harvest people. Some of us will be caught up to heaven like grain stalks cut from the ground, freed from the root system that chained us to this earth, ready to be presented to God amid the swirling aroma of fresh-baked bread.

There are others, though, who will never experience this kind of joy and freedom. Their future holds nothing but the foul sight of grapes being smashed in a winepress—like houseflies "splatted" on a windowpane, like watermelons dropped from a third story balcony—their blood flowing four feet deep in every direction. Death everywhere, with no place to hide—and even worse things to come.

? Why would God choose to be so violently descriptive about His end-time judgment? Is this something we should want to tell people? Would they listen if we did?

_____

_____

_____

_____

Drama Recap

So the drama that began in chapter 12 reaches its earthly end. History began with God choosing a people (the "woman" of 12:1), from whom He would send His Son, their Savior, into the world. Satan's business from then until now has been to "wage war" against the people of God (12:17). This will never be more visible than when he trots out his antichrist and false prophet to try winning the world through economic, political, and religious domination.

When it's all said and done, however, all who have followed the evil one will find themselves here . . . piled high in the winepress, crushed under the weight of unforgiven sin, helpless against the blows of God's righteous wrath . . . while those who have trusted Christ will find themselves in His glorious presence forever.

Now, as chapter 15 begins, get ready to say good-bye to the world—one bowl at a time.

Revelation 15

15:1-4 Another Break in the Action

Sort of picking up where chapter 11 left off—before the drama of chapters 12–14—we apparently step back into real time, where preparations are underway for the seven final judgments.

But before things really get hopping, we must gear up with one of our well-known interludes (like chapters 7 and 10), as "another great and awe-inspiring sign" appears in heaven (verse 1). Seven angels move into position to receive the last, trembling containers of God's wrath, His final blow against the curse of sin. The crystal sea of heaven is said to be "mixed with fire," reflecting the red-hot glow of judgment.

Meanwhile, the redeemed are free to focus on God, their Deliverer, having been rescued from the judgment they once deserved, saved by faith in the forgiving blood of Christ (verse 2).

What a contrast, huh? The world hurries to lock its doors against the plagues of end-time judgment, while the

HARPS.
Similar to the lyre (the instrument used by David), the harp was the stringed instrument more commonly associated with the aristocracy. It was usually made of precious woods or metals and generally appeared in sacred settings, for religious uses.

SONG OF MOSES.
This refers to two recorded songs in Moses' writings: one following the parting of the Red Sea in Exodus 15:1-18, and the other delivered just prior to Moses' death (Deuteronomy 32:1-43), reflecting on God's faithful guidance and protection.

BOWLS.
The Greek word used here for "bowl" is specifically a bowl used in offerings. This shows that these judgments of God—as crushing as they are—are altogether righteous and holy.

TABERNACLE.
This movable tent structure—like a church on wheels—was the portable worship center for the Israelites throughout their many years of wandering from place to place. The cloud of God's presence descended on it when they were stationary, then lifted to lead them to their next destination (Exodus 40:34-38). It was replaced by the temple, built during Solomon's reign, constructed along the same design and consisting of the same worship elements.

resurrected believers sway to the sounds of string music. They sing of God's . . .

- Works—His incredible power on display in saving them as well as dealing with sin
- Righteousness—His absolute, one hundred percent purity in both actions and motive
- Truth—His right to perform all His mighty acts, based on His eternal, unchanging Word
- Name—His ability to live up to His title, to be the God He claims to be
- Holiness—His total supremacy over every rival, His distinction as the one true God

15:5-8 Bowl Prep

Have you ever tried carrying a bowl or bucket through the house that was filled to the top with some kind of sloshing stuff, like water for the dog, or suds for washing your car? What about with ashes from the fireplace? If you're not careful with those, clouds of dust and residue can poof into the air and onto the carpet with every step.

So imagine the flight of these seven angels, entrusted with the "seven gold bowls filled with the wrath of God" (verse 7). Imagine the fear, awe, and reverence they feel as they receive their assignments in the inner sanctum of God's presence. Imagine the tension as they await the command to whisk their frothing bowls quickly out of heaven's atmosphere, then down to the earth, already creaking and groaning from the hammer blows of previous judgments.

Trailing behind them is the smoke of God's glory—perhaps to shield the believers' eyes from the full-on destruction of the earth, but certainly to overshadow His people's thoughts with worship, praise, and the amazing reality that they are safe with Him forever.

Verse 8. Why would God, while waiting for the "seven plagues" to be administered, bar the door to His presence? We're not sure. But keep in mind that God doesn't need us. He wasn't feeling bored and incomplete the day He decided to create the world. The Father, Son, and Holy Spirit are and have always been perfectly content and sustained by their own existence. It is by God's love, mercy, and grace alone—not by the cute way our dimples look when we grin at Him—that He has welcomed us into His presence. Yes, He loves us. Yes, He paid sin's price for us. But never forget that God is bigger than the biggest thought we could ever have about Him. He has received us as His children, but He stands alone as the great God of glory.

Why is a proper relationship with God mixed with equal parts of fear and love? How do you experience these two aspects and emotions in your life with Him?

_____

_____

_____

_____

Revelation 16

One of the characteristics of the trumpet judgments was that they were partial. Remember how it sometimes said they affected "a third" of the trees or the oceans or the sky? They continued to leave open the possibility that people would "see and fear, and put their trust in the LORD" (Psalm 40:3).

These bowl judgments, however, are total and complete. You can sense the finality in the way they pour down. Again, though—just like before—the first four have a direct impact on the earth, while the others reach out to destroy spiritual forces.

16:1-2 Bowl #1—Painful Sores

Have you ever had one of those painful little canker sores inside your mouth? Man, those can hurt. You bite them by accident when you're eating. Your toothpaste stings them. Tell you what—in case you're not suffering with one right now, be sure to thank God for giving you a day of relief.

Praying for relief won't be an option, however, for the people who've spent their final days following the antichrist and worshiping "his image" (verse 2). When the first bowl judgment begins breaking out all over their bodies, these "severely painful sores" will give them *another* set of distinguishing marks to go along with the "mark of the beast" they've been wearing.

16:3 Bowl #2—Total Ocean Destruction

If you've ever done any deep-sea fishing or have been around the place where they clean and pack them, you know what a rank, putrid stench comes from dead, rotting fish (and fish parts). Imagine that smell being everywhere! Imagine watching the waves roll in, red with the blood of its underwater creatures, pounding the surf with huge clumps of their heavy carcasses.

When the second trumpet blew in 8:8-9, "a third of the sea became blood, a third of the living creatures in the sea died, and a third of the ships were destroyed." But when the contents of the second bowl hits the oceans, "all life in the sea" is going to die. All of it. Everywhere.

16:4-7 Bowl #3—Blood on the River

Have you ever wanted revenge? Have you ever had your neighbor hate you because you're having your friends over for Bible study? Have you ever been singled out as a goody two-shoes? Has one of your parents ever been persecuted at work for taking an ethical stand, and you wanted to lash out against the ones who were making life difficult for your mom or dad?

The Bible specifically teaches us, of course, that we are not allowed to avenge ourselves on others. But God alone is justified in defending Himself and His people. "'Vengeance belongs to Me; I will repay,' says the Lord" (Romans 12:9).

When the third angel upends his bowl, then, causing all the earth's freshwater to swim in its own blood, turning every cupful of drinking water into a kill-me-dead cocktail, those who "poured out the blood of the saints and prophets" in death will have nothing but blood to pour out of their household pitchers. The punishment will fit the crime.

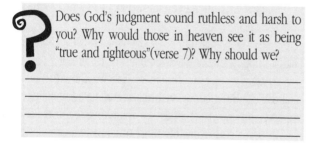

Does God's judgment sound ruthless and harsh to you? Why would those in heaven see it as being "true and righteous"(verse 7)? Why should we?

JUDGMENT.

We tend to think of judgment as bad and ugly, but the Psalm writers often prayed for judgment or justice as a desirable thing. They wrote as Israelites who were frequent victims of injustice, who had been abused and mistreated by other people and nations. Judgment to them was an appeal for God to make things right, to defend their cause. They wanted "justice" to "again be righteous" [Psalm 94:15] and not used corruptly against them to meet others' needs.

16:8-9 Bowl #4—Red-Hot Sunburns

By now, we're expecting the people who are being bowled over with God's wrath to start giving up, surrendering, declaring Him the winner and acknowledging His supremacy in the power department. Does it surprise you, then, to see them responding to the scorching heat of a juiced-up sun, not with white flags and their hands up, but with curses and clenched fists?

Maybe it shouldn't. The last time you were disciplined by your parents, or called down at youth group, or singled out for punishment after an incident in the halls after school, were you quick to apologize and to see things their way? Or did it take you a while to quit making excuses, trying to blame your mom and dad or some other authority figure for picking on you and making such a big deal out of this?

THE SUN.

We don't think about it much, but the sun, you know, is indescribably hot and dangerous. Tilt it a fraction of a degree in the wrong direction, and it either leaves us without enough heat or with way more than we can handle. The sun itself is one great example of how God cares for all people on earth, saved and unsaved alike. He has placed the sun in its precise location to make life on earth livable. It's not surprising that some ancient people worshiped the sun for its power. We should see the sun's properties and capabilities and worship its Creator.

HEAT EXCHANGE.
Notice the big difference between the recipients of the fourth bowl, "burned by the intense heat" [verse 9], and the redeemed who live in heaven, where "no longer will the sun strike them, or any heat" [7:16].

LUCIFER.
One of the boldest descriptions of Satan's deceptiveness is that he is an "angel of light" [2 Corinthians 11:14]. One of his names, in fact—Lucifer—means "light-bearer" and comes from Isaiah 14:12, where the Devil is seen as a "shining morning star." In light of the fourth bowl, however, we see how dark his future really is.

DARKNESS.
One of the reasons the plague of darkness was so shocking on ancient Egypt [Exodus 10:21-23] was because their primary deity was Re or Ra [pronounced RAY], the sun god. For him not to show up for several days was a good way to defuse an idolater.

Again, this is how deceptive Satan is—not just in this future-tense setting but right now. It's astounding what he can convince us to do and to think.

16:10-11 Bowl #5—All Dark in the Devil's Den

Except for some who are a little scared of the dark or like to sleep with a nightlight, we don't worry about darkness too much, since we have flashlights and candles and the promise of the sun coming up in the morning. But have you ever been in a place so dark—like when exploring an underground cave or lost on a country road—that you really feared for your safety? You know what that kind of darkness feels like.

Perhaps with this fifth-bowl darkness, however, we're talking about something that's not just black air but a darkness that has weight and heaviness to it. We know that this final-day darkness comes with the accumulated weight of four previous bowls of judgment—painful sores, contaminated oceans and rivers, burning-hot temperatures—all of which make the eerie uncertainty of the blackness even more terrifying and severe.

Not severe enough, though, to generate any kind of repentant response from the people of the beast. They gnaw "their tongues from pain" whenever they aren't busy spitting cuss words in God's direction.

> **?** Did you know there are people who—on their deathbeds, in their last moments, with no hope of survival at all—will not use even their final breath to call out to Jesus? Why?
>
> _____
>
> _____
>
> _____

16:12-16 Bowl #6—Preparing for Armageddon

A couple of things to pick up from this passage:

• *Satan's limits.* When we think about seeing the Devil, the antichrist, and the false prophet coming at us all at once, vomiting out these slimy, demonic frogs that are powerful enough to pounce into a king's presence and coerce him into coalition with Satan's forces, we're talking horror movie. We're talking about running screaming into the hills or dropping dead right where we stand. We see no way to defeat a horde like that. This is ultimate fear factor.

But what does God do? He dries up the river so these guys can have an easier time getting across. So we ask you: Is God quivering in His boots, shaking like a leaf just because the Devil is amassing his monsters and training every weapon known to man against the forces of heaven?

• *God's total control.* No, God is not worried. Rather than recoiling from the booms, flares, and clashes of these underworld armies, God goes on the offensive. Saying basically the same thing Jesus said in Luke 12:39-40, He announces to all people that, if Satan wants to bang around and flex his muscles, let him knock himself out all he wants to. God's plan is still going forward on His timetable, at the effortless snap of His mighty fingers—and no diddly devil can do anything to stop it.

ARMAGEDDON.
Pronounced "ARM-uh-GEDD-un," this is the site of the final battle between the forces of good and evil. The word itself is a Greek treatment of the Hebrew word that means "mountain of Megiddo," an ancient Middle Eastern city where as many as 200 bloody battles were fought.

FROGS.
Because the frog was an unclean animal to the Jews and was also a symbol of Persian and Egyptian gods and goddesses, it was a doubly unclean, apt description of satanic spirits.

16:17-21 Bowl #7—"It Is Done"

Sometimes—just to sell tickets—a little II-A college football team will put a major, national powerhouse on their schedule. The small-time players and coaches will tell each other that anything can happen, that the Big U boys put on their uniform pants one leg at a time, just like everybody else. They'll pump the locker room with pre-game, chest-pounding noise, then roar onto the field with the 0-to-0 scoreboard behind them, as if to give credence to their equality.

"IT IS DONE!"
Kind of makes you think of Jesus' final words on the cross, doesn't it? "It is finished!" (John 19:30). When God says "it is done," you can take it to the bank. It's done.

EARTHQUAKES.
The land that makes up modern-day Israel has historically endured two to three major quakes every century, as well as two to six minor shocks a year. The Bible refers to a big one in Amos 1:1 and Zechariah 14:5, not to mention the ones that occurred at Jesus' death and resurrection.

But then the game starts. The skinny legs from State College find out real quick why the big boys play on New Year's Day.

When Satan trots his troops onto the Armageddon battlefield—only to see the battlefield itself splintering from an earthquake "like no other since man has been on the earth" (verse 18)—the world will finally see that they've tangled with the wrong God. The battle of Armageddon may sound like the ultimate in head-to-head, hand-to-hand combat, with the momentum swinging one way and the other, with the fate of the world hanging on whichever one emerges as victor.

If that's been your impression, then read verses 17-21 again. Does it still sound like a back-and-forth battle to you now? No, this isn't even a fair fight.

So God booms from His throne, "It is done." Truer words have never been spoken. Though it's been this way from the very beginning, the time will come when everyone will know that Satan is toast . . . and God is King.

> Seeing the earth splitting into shattered parts, with the islands and mountains sinking into the sea, does it make you wonder, "What earthly things do I place way too much confidence in?"
>
> _____
>
> _____
>
> _____
>
> _____

End of the Second Vision

The last verse of chapter 16 wraps up the second vision of Revelation, which began in the throne room of heaven (4:1) and concludes here with the total destruction of the earth and its unbelieving inhabitants.

The third vision (out of four) begins with chapter 17 and runs through 21:8, reviewing the same end-time events we've just witnessed, only from a different perspective, with more dialogue and detail. It results (of course) in the same dead end for the Devil—and the same victory lap for the redeemed.

Put yourself in biology class, with a microscope sitting on the desk between you and your lab partner. The teacher asks you to yank a single hair out of your head and place it on a slide under the microscope lens. *A hair? What's to see in a human hair?* But when you look into the view finder, you discover a lot more going on than you expected. You see texture and complexity and weight and dimension.

This next vision of Revelation—from 17:1 to 21:8—is like twisting the magnifying wheel on a microscope, zooming in on the images and emotions that make up the final days of earth's existence. This is not what happens immediately following the bowl judgments. This is just a different way of seeing what it will be like in the middle of them.

17:1-6 The Prostitute and the Scarlet Beast

The Prostitute Introduced (verses 1-2)

What makes up the motivations and emotions of impure sex—the kind that occurs between boyfriends and girlfriends, between camp counselors and coworkers, or even between perfect strangers?

- Selfishness—wanting what I want
- Pleasure—wanting to feel good
- Approval—wanting to be desirable
- Acceptance—wanting to feel special
- Immediate gratification—wanting it now

But don't these all apply to every other unholy desire in life? When you're jealous of what others have? When you're greedy for more money? When you're wanting to beat one particular guy or girl in a school election?

So when God introduces "the notorious prostitute" into the Revelation scene—whether she be the Roman empire of John's day, the Babylon of the last day, or the immoral,

PROSTITUTION.
This trading of sexual services for pay goes back to the earliest days of civilization. It has always resulted from the double standard of men wanting their daughters and wives to be pure while desiring access to other women. The idea of cult prostitution also shows up in the Bible, where sexual acts were considered part of a pagan religious experience.

MANY WATERS.
This phrase from verse 1 brings to mind the description of Babylon in Jeremiah 51:13. The cup in her hand is also part of this vision, where the nations are seen as being drunk on Babylon's filth (Jeremiah 51:6-7). Actually, this entire chapter of Jeremiah is worth reading alongside Revelation 17.

PURPLE AND SCARLET.
These two colors were among those associated with wealth, royalty, and luxury in the ancient world. Scarlet dye was obtained from the shield louse. This insect was killed, crushed, and dissolved in water. It took lots of these insects to make scarlet dye. For this reason, it was expensive and was worn by the wealthy. Scarlet was a prominent color in the tabernacle (Exodus 25:4; 26:1), Aaron's vestment, and the veil in Solomon's temple (2 Chronicles 3:14). Scarlet dye was stubborn, hard to remove. It's this property of scarlet that links it with sin. But God's grace and power are able to do what is otherwise impossible. "Though your sins are like scarlet, they will be as white as snow" (Isaiah 1:18).

cultural climate that entices us every day—He's describing more than sexual temptation. He's talking about the tug of every earthly, temporary pleasure, the allure of power, the desire to want more, to have more, to be bigger and more important than everyone else. We all feel it. But we don't have to fall for it.

The Prostitute in Action (verses 3-6)

What's the one underlying theme that runs through just about every TV show, every movie, every music video, every Super Bowl commercial, every top 40 song, every comedian's big laugh, every time you turn around?

No wonder, then, that this passage contains some of the most sexually provocative language and images in the whole Bible. It paints a picture of the gluttonies and excesses that always been the downfall of even the greatest empires and cultures.

Sexual temptation promises so much. It drapes itself in fun and Friday nights and airbrushed perfection. But look what the "scarlet beast" is hoping you don't see. Look what the devilish dragon "covered with blasphemous names" doesn't want you to know until you're already hooked. Look at the woman—the one who represents all the seductions of sexual desire and every other ungodly pursuit.

- She's tacky—covered in bold colors and gaudy jewelry
- She's drunk—her "gold cup" filled with "everything vile"
- She's unapologetic—proudly displaying her well-earned reputation
- She hates both you and your God—and everything He stands for

Boys, is she who you really want to exchange a loving relationship with the Lord for? Girls, is he who you really want?

John was "astounded" when he saw sin in all its hideousness. Why aren't we? Is it because we've grown too accustomed to it? Because we're not convinced God has something better for us?

_____

_____

_____

_____

17:7-17 The Interpretation

Who Is the Beast? (verses 7-14)

A lot of this isn't easy to understand. Fortunately, of course, there won't be a test at the gates of heaven on this. God certainly won't hold us accountable for our grasp of every detail, especially when so many of them are really unknowable.

But let's at least give it a shot, shall we?

There were basically five empires (see *Empires* below) in ancient history—"five have fallen" (verse 10)—followed by Rome, the sixth world empire, the one in power at the time John was writing this. No doubt, the "seven mountains" or "seven hills" (verse 9) were a direct reference to Rome's main geographical feature.

The seventh empire "has not yet come" (verse 10), but when it does, it will soon be overtaken by the antichrist—the "beast"—for the purposes of Satan, making his final empire "the eighth" (verse 11) and the last to dominate the world.

Somewhere along the line, "ten kings" will join forces with the antichrist's empire, united in purpose to "make war against the Lamb" (verse 14) and against those of us who are allied with Him. No one knows for sure who these kings and kingdoms will be.

But two things we do know:

• *Satan's "destruction" is sure* (verse 8). His beast will one day "come up from the abyss," dragging all kinds of military might, political pressure, and brute force into his

BABYLON THE GREAT.
Again, this literal yet representative city is symbolic of man's decadence and God's judgment. Throughout Revelation, when taking into account the historical setting of the book, it's pretty clear that Rome is in view. Who knows what "city" it represents today?

ELECT.
These are the people of God, who have entered into special relationship with Him through His Son, Jesus Christ. They have been known by Him "before the foundation of the world" [Ephesians 1:4] and will remain His possession throughout all eternity. They do not include those "whose names were not written in the book of life" [verse 8].

EMPIRES.
There were basically five empires in ancient history: Egypt, Assyria, Babylon, Persia, and Greece. Rome became the sixth. Who will be the seventh? Good question.

THE BEAST.
Take a closer look at the beast and these chaotic, climactic world events in Daniel 7:19-27. See the identical descriptions, too, between verse 7 and the antichrist in 13:1.

THE PROSTITUTE'S DESTRUCTION.
For a more complete, descriptive account of the prostitute's demise, read the prophecy from Ezekiel 23:11-35.

THE WATERS.
Just about all major cities have been situated on water. Even the big cities in America primarily grew up around the inflow and outflow of trade on the rivers and seaports.

cause. His cause, however, is doomed to failure.

- *"The Lamb will conquer them"* (verse 14). No matter who Satan draws into collusion against the armies of heaven, he and his henchmen will be defeated by none other than the risen Christ, who needs no other power or world alliance to do His fighting for Him.

Who Is the Prostitute? (verses 15-18)

Prior to the aggressions of Adolf Hitler that became World War II, the Nazi tyrant convinced Joseph Stalin (dictator of the former Soviet Union) to sign a non-aggression pact with Germany, promising that however much territory either nation gobbled up, they would never attack each other.

But little more than two years after putting his signature on paper—June 1941—Hitler launched one of his famous blitzkriegs against the Soviet Union. Betrayal and broken promises are the stock-in-trade of ruthless leaders. Should we expect any more of the Devil himself and his antichrist?

Verse 16. According to this passage, the "beast" will grow to hate the "prostitute." She is identified in verse 18 as the anti-God spirit that infiltrated ancient Babylon, first-century Rome, and every culture that has rejected its Creator and sworn allegiance to human lust and power.

This is what the Devil and his demons are like. We've seen it before in Revelation, and we see it again in this description of satanic civil war. He not only hates believers; he even hates those who follow him and carry out his orders. He's a hater, a murderer, who will make the prostitute "desolate and naked, devour her flesh, and burn her up with fire" (verse 16). He destroys everything he touches.

> Have you seen the destructive forces of Satan at work in your life? In your family? In your school? In your church even? How? Has he ever failed to fail you?
>
> _____
>
> _____
>
> _____
>
> _____

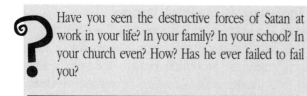

Revelation 18

18:1-8 The Fall of Babylon

Judgment on the Great City (verses 1-3)

Sin, once it's had its way with you, always leaves you in a prison of guilt and dead ends. Perhaps you've gotten to where it's easy for you to lie, and as a result you've been trapped between so many different stories, nobody believes anything you say anymore. Perhaps you've played around with drugs and alcohol, and now you're lured to the beer cooler every time you walk into the convenience store for gum and a gas fill-up.

When "Babylon the Great" finally falls—the last, powerfully prosperous city, the center of false religion and global commerce—it's going to become a prison. All its gleaming skyscrapers, fancy hotels, and neon entertainment districts will become a "haunt" for everything "unclean" and undesirable. All those who became drunk on "the wine of her sexual immorality," who grew "wealthy from her excessive luxury" (verse 3), will be chained inside forever with the demons of lust and violence and every sick addiction known to man.

"It has fallen, Babylon the great has fallen!" It's the only destination our sin can ever deliver.

UNCLEAN ANIMALS.
God gave a specific listing of clean and unclean animals to ancient Israel, and the people's revulsion at unclean birds and beasts persisted into John's day. Read this interesting list for yourself in Leviticus 11.

WIDOWS.

These [along with orphans] were considered the most helpless members of ancient society. In a culture so centered around the family, the woman who had no husband often became a social misfit with no one to provide for her or to represent her interests in the courts. "Babylon the Great" never dreamed of a day when she would need anyone else to support her.

GOD'S MEMORY.

Our Father in His mercy chooses to forget our sins. For "if You considered sins," the psalmist wrote, "Lord, who could stand?" (Psalm 130:3). Yet while God has removed our sins from us "as far as the east is from the west" (Psalm 103:12), He does not forget the sins of the unredeemed and unrepentant. They are "piled up to heaven. . . . God has remembered" (verses 5-6). Someone you know may need to hear that soon.

The Escape of God's People (verses 4-8)

Have you ever known someone who lost everything "in one day"? Sometimes you'll hear of a family whose house was demolished in a tornado. You'll see them on the news, picking through their rain-soaked belongings, wondering how they can ever rebuild. Sometimes a person whose fortune is built on debt and speculation can watch their finances drain into the tank on one day's slide in the stock market. Ask the person whose father died in a freak accident at work if one day can change your whole life.

One of these days in Babylon, that's what it's going to come down to. One day. And however much fun and games some people had with life, their bill is going to come due at double the payment (verse 6). It'll be like everything costing twice as much, yet giving you nothing but trouble in return.

But while God is punishing sin—even this late in the tribulation period—He will still be saving sinners. There will still be those who are counted among His people, believers in Christ, forced to survive the horrific climate of the last day.

They will be assured, however, that they will be spared from "her plagues" (verse 4). God's command to them is that they must not "share in her sins," must not give in or give up, but must keep believing in their sure hope—their coming King and His eternal kingdom.

> Do you know someone who has the same attitude as the people of Babylon—"I will never see grief" (verse 7)—who feels untouchable, indestructible? How can you help them see the truth?
>
> _____
> _____
> _____
> _____

18:9-20 Reactions to the Fall

It doesn't matter what it is—a major league baseball game, a music awards show, a talk show interview—you always want to hear what the participants had to say about it. *What was it like? What made the difference? What do you have to say to your fans?* And the ever-popular: *How does it feel?*

In this passage—while Babylon burns—the angelic reporters fan out into the various neighborhoods and side streets, gauging public opinion about this downturn of events.

• *First, we hear from the kings* (verses 9-10). Moving as far as they can get from Babylon's borders, these leaders of other cities and countries now keep their distance, lest the fires of judgment reach their personal property. At one time they enjoyed dabbling in Babylon's lust and luxury. They liked rubbing shoulders with the rich and famous, the elite of society. But now all they can do is grieve her fall. They are in sheer disbelief that their day at the top of the world has come crashing down.

• *Next, we hear from the business community* (verses 11-17a). Don't read any real sorrow into their words. The only sadness they feel toward the fall of Babylon is the loss of their profits. For years they made a mint by supplying the city's insatiable appetite for gold and silver, for fancy food and furniture, even for "human bodies and souls"—most likely, her dependence on the slave trade. Just as the city is in ruins, so are their revenues and retirement accounts.

• *Finally, we hear from the sailors* (verses 17b-20). Again, their lament is not genuine sympathy, but rather disappointment at the loss of business, at no longer having sex available at every port of call. They do seem to understand, however, that her punishment is valid and well-deserved. They know that this is not merely a bad set of circumstances but a sure judgment from the living God—a judgment that's been many years and martyrs in the making.

GLOBAL CALAMITY.
Some people dismiss this kind of worldwide destruction as absurd. But we already see today how interrelated the commerce, banking, and computer systems of the world have become. Mom-and-Pop stores are being forced from business by huge chains and discounters with centralized operations. Add to this the "mark of the beast" procedure for acquiring goods and services, and it's not too hard to imagine how Babylon could fall in a day.

DUST.
Throwing dust or ashes on your head (verse 19) was a common, ancient expression of sorrow and repentance (Isaiah 58:5; Daniel 9:3). It wasn't unusual, though, for these outward signs of grief over sin to become nothing but a show.

MILLSTONES.
These were two circular stones that spun against one another to grind grain into flour. Each solid stone was usually 2–4 inches thick and about a foot and a half in diameter, made of basalt and heavy as all get-out.

SORCERY.
The psychic practice of trying to use supernatural powers to gain wisdom and ascertain the future was refined to an unholy art form by the Babylonians (Ezekiel 21:21).

COMMERCE.
The lists of cargo and merchandise from this passage are similar to the items mentioned in Ezekiel 16:9-13 as well as 27:5-24.

18:21-24 Good-Bye Babylon

There's an old episode of *The Waltons*—a classic television drama from the 1970s—where John-Boy, the oldest son in a large mountain family, is preparing to leave home and go to college. He's up in his room one evening, talking to his mother about what he's going to miss most about not being around the house anymore. (If you're preparing to leave home soon yourself, or already have, you'll be able to relate.)

He says it's not the big things he'll miss. Instead, it's the little ordinary sights and sounds of everyday life—hearing his parents talking quietly about the day's events as he lay in bed at night, the sound of dishes rattling in the kitchen every morning, the familiar view out the front window.

Truly, it's the things we see and experience every day—almost without noticing—that bring a settled security to life. But imagine never again being able to . . .

• Hear another note of music
• Go into your favorite store
• See your dad pull up in the driveway after work
• Read by the light of your bedside lamp
• Attend the wedding of a friend—or have any hope of marrying

Hundreds of these "never agains" are coming one day to a city near you, as Babylon the Great becomes Babylon the Grounded. Hurled like "a large millstone . . . into the sea" (verse 21), it will disappear in an instant, the waters of time settling over its sinking spot as if it never existed.

Among its citizens were some of the best and brightest, "the nobility of the earth" (verse 23), but they wasted all their talents and potential on things that could neither last nor satisfy. They bludgeoned God's people into heaven, thinking they were ridding the world of intolerance, only to find that they were sending themselves to a hell of eternal intolerance.

Sad, isn't it? But for the vast "multitude in heaven" (19:1), who can't get enough of God anymore, this is only right. God is claiming His final victory over sin and death.

Revelation 19

19:1-5 Heaven's Reaction

This is the pep rally in the gym at 2:00. It's the clock winding down on the scoreboard, the crush of friends and fans racing onto the field after your school wins the state championship. It's the caps-in-the-air fling of graduation day. It's the celebration of a hard-won victory. It's over. It's over! It's finally over!

The singers who pack the stage at this Fall-of-Babylon party are probably the same ones we heard from in 7:9-10—the redeemed of every nation, including those who had been murdered during the great tribulation. Alongside are our old friends "the 24 elders and the four living creatures" (4:4-8), as well as other angelic and heavenly beings. And they're all saying the same thing: "Hallelujah . . . praise our God . . . because His judgments are true and righteous."

HALLELUJAH.
This is an exclamation of praise that shows up frequently in the book of Psalms and in other sections of worship verse in the Scripture. It means "praise Yahweh," which is the Hebrew name for the covenant-keeping, truth-telling God.

Verse 2. The mood in heaven seems striking to our modern ears. We'd really expect the redeemed to be sad that so many are suffering for their sins. And they are! We should be! God is. He wants "everyone to be saved and to come to the knowledge of the truth" (1 Timothy 2:4). He has been waiting and waiting and waiting until this time of final judgment, "not wanting any to perish, but all to come to repentance" (2 Peter 3:9). Yet all have been given ample opportunity. Everyone has been warned and invited. When it all shakes out, we must choose to celebrate God's righteousness, trusting in His mercy, fairness, and judgment.

THE BRIDE.
The unique relationship between a man and woman in marriage is often used as a biblical picture of the Lord with His people. You see it in places like Jeremiah 13:1-14, the first three chapters of Hosea, and Ephesians 5:22-33.

SPIRIT OF PROPHECY.
Although biblical prophecy covers a lot of ground and talks about a lot of things, the truth about Jesus Christ is its central message, greatest hope, and recurring theme. Check out Isaiah 53 and Daniel 7:13-14 for some clear examples.

WEDDINGS.
On the day of a wedding in Bible-times Israel, the groom and his friends would dress up and go to the bride's house, carrying her back to his home with singing and dancing. After vows were exchanged, the newlyweds would go inside and consummate the marriage while the guests waited outside. Friends would continue coming and going for up to a week following the wedding, feasting, partying, and celebrating.

19:6-10 The Marriage of the Lamb

Ah, weddings! It's going to be you one day, most likely—walking down the aisle in a misty glow of white, or watching your bride approach you, more beautiful than you've ever seen her. The music, the ceremony, the vows, the flower girl, the candles, the rings, the kiss, the cake, the pictures, the honeymoon, the life you've always wanted.

But there's a day in your future that's sure to be even more special and spectacular than the most perfect of wedding days—the marriage of the Lamb with His bride, the church.

When He first found us, we were hardly the marrying type. We were filthy, disgusting, our wedding clothes deeply stained with our own sin—ground-in dirt, impossible to get out even with our best attempts at washing them. Yet somehow—for some reason—He still desired us. He still wanted us.

When He looked into our eyes, we did our best to apologize for the sorry shape we were in. We looked down at ourselves . . . knowing He knew. What we saw instead—to our wild surprise—was "fine linen, bright and pure" (verse 8), the reflection of His glowing presence surrounding us in light. The One we never deserved had made us worthy of His affections.

Never forget how wonderful this is!

It's enough to make you want to put the person who brings this reality alive for you on a pedestal—the way John did to his angelic host. But there's no pastor, no youth pastor, no famous evangelist, no college friend, no praying parent, no superstar with the incredible Christian testimony to thank for this good news. This is Jesus' work, start to finish. When you think about the prospect of this wonderful wedding day, worship the Lamb!

Verse 8. Likely you've always thought we were made righteous by the grace of God, not by our "righteous acts." Yes, you're right. But even though we Christians can be lazy with our faith at times and commit our fair share of *un*righteous acts, the change of heart Jesus gave us at salvation *will result* in an overall lifetime of changed behavior, a noticeable difference from the world. So keep getting up after every fall. What starts with God's grace will sooner or later, little by little, become a "fine linen" way of life. Believe it.

19:11-16 The White Horse Rider

Even with all the dazzling marriage talk from the last section, we're still not totally out of the bloody part yet. But it's time to close our eyes and imagine this warm-up to the end: See the gates of heaven opening (verse 11). Hear the gasps, claps, and shouts of joy traveling like waves through the crowd, turning our attention toward a majestic "white horse" whose rider is called "Faithful and True," who bears His triumphant title on His sleeve: "King of kings and Lord of lords" (verse 16).

Behind Him ride the armies of heaven "wearing pure white linen" on their own white horses (verse 14)—not because He needs their help to defeat His enemies, but just because He wants them to join Him in celebrating His victory.

Yes, there is still judgment to be measured out:

- His robe is "stained" with the "blood" of the unrighteous (verse 13).
- His holy Word severs everything opposed to His truth (verse 15).
- His feet trample those who doubt the "fierce anger of God" (verse 15).

But the end is near. Our most fearsome foes are nearly crushed. The freedom of full victory is just around the corner.

UNKNOWN.
Oddly enough, there are some things we may never know—even in heaven—like the "name" mentioned in verse 12. People often say, "When I get to heaven, the first thing I'm going to ask Jesus is . . ." and then mention some rare bit of mysterious biblical trivia. But even in heaven, apparently, some mysteries that we don't need to know will always remain with God. That should make it easier for us not to feel the need to know everything now.

JESUS AS JUDGE.
Some of the Old Testament passages that speak of God as judge and deliverer are Psalms 50:16-23 and 59:1-17.

JEZEBEL.
This wicked queen of Israel's King Ahab ended up in this same kind of mess when she was killed in 2 Kings 9:30-37. Her name, like Babylon's, is synonymous with evil and godlessness.

FINAL BATTLE.
The scenes from verses 19-21 should be seen as a parallel passage to the Armageddon battle of 16:16. This final war doesn't seem to have multiple phases like this, although that's how it kind of looks if you read Revelation straight through chronologically.

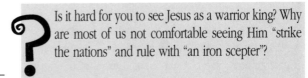

Is it hard for you to see Jesus as a warrior king? Why are most of us not comfortable seeing Him "strike the nations" and rule with "an iron scepter"?

_____

_____

_____

19:17-21 Victory in Battle

The Fate of Satan's Armies (verses 17-18)

Few things are much grosser than road kill. Of course, it gets a good bit grosser when you see a bunch of crows and blackbirds picking the gooey parts out of the fur, the bugs swarming around what's left of a dead squirrel or rabbit or raccoon or deer.

Still, nothing must compare to a sight we've hopefully never seen—vultures coming to scavenge the bodies of dead people.

By the time all of God's judgments and terrors have inflicted His wrath on the world, by the time Jesus rides His white horse in triumph over all the God-haters, by the time Armageddon has ended in utter defeat, the landscape will be littered with the "flesh of kings . . . of commanders . . . of mighty men . . . of everyone, both free and slave, small and great" (verse 18).

Without exception, those who won't be attending the "marriage feast of the Lamb" (verse 9) will be on the menu at the "great supper of God" (verse 17).

The Fate of the Antichrist and the False Prophet (verses 19-21)

There are people who died today who never thought for a moment that driving drunk was beyond their capabilities. There are people who were diagnosed with sexually transmitted diseases today who never dreamed they would contract one themselves. There are people who lost their spot on the school team today for flaunting the rules who never saw it coming.

The "beast" with all his multinational armies and the "false prophet" with all his magical powers will never expect their battle to end this way—"taken prisoner" and then "thrown alive into the lake of fire"—without so much as firing a shot. They'll go down arrogantly believing they had the ability to win.

But that's the way their wicked reign will end. Their weapons will be no match for the singular, simple word that comes from Jesus' mouth. Their deception will be thwarted by truth, and their destiny will be sealed forever.

LEADERSHIP.
One of the truths that God has fashioned into our earthly experience is that leaders are held accountable. Just as teachers are responsible not only for their own actions and attitudes but also for those of the people who are influenced by them (James 3:1), it's only fitting that the antichrist should be dealt with first. Those who lead others into sin should be the first to taste its bitter fruit.

Revelation 20

The Millennium

All right, this chapter brings us to the spot where most of the opinions and interpretations of Revelation are based: the Millennium (mill-IN-ee-um)—the 1,000-year reign of Christ. The main issue hinges around the question of when Jesus Christ will return in relation to the millennium.

So this chapter is where a lot of the Revelation labels get applied. And here they are:

• *Premillennial*—Those who hold to this view believe that at Satan's defeat, that's when Jesus will appear and establish a literal kingdom of God on earth, with Him as our King—on this planet—for a thousand years. Inside this viewpoint, there are two main camps:

• *Historic premillennialism*, which sees believers being resurrected at the beginning of the millennium to reign with Christ. Nonbelievers, then, are resurrected after the millennium, followed by the final judgment.

• *Dispensational premillennialism*. There are variations on this theme, but its primary beliefs are that the church will be "raptured" (taken up) prior to the seven-year tribulation, escaping all the judgments and everything, returning with Christ in glory at the end of that time to reign with Him for a thousand years and restore God's covenant with Israel.

• *Amillennial*—(pronounced AH-mill-in-ial). This view maintains that we are living in the millennial reign of Christ right now, since He is already reigning in heaven. Once Satan and his kingdom are visibly destroyed (chapter 20), all believers will then rise to reign with Jesus.

• *Postmillennial*—In this framework, the millennium is seen as a period of great evangelism. The Spirit will unusually energize Christian preaching and teaching, the church will be purified, and many will be converted by the appeal of the gospel. Then Christ will return for His people.

You got all that?

20:1-3 Satan's Defeat

Imagine living a whole day with no Satan to tempt you. No pressure to ignore anybody. No competition over this boy or that girl. No need to look better than anyone else. No addictions. No illusions. No tricks, traps, or guilt trips. Wouldn't that be great?

CHAINS.
Most examples of chains in biblical history have to do with decoration, ornamentation, jewelry styles, and architectural devices. But the heavier, much more rugged variety were used to prevent prisoners from escaping.

One day, he really is going into the tank—into the "abyss," locked down with a "great chain," sealed off from any access to those he so loved to deceive. It won't take a hundred angels to do the job—not even an elite group from the highest ranks—just one ordinary angel "coming down from heaven" jingling his keychain. (Satan deserves that kind of humiliation.)

This is not his final destination, however. This is more like a prison, a sin-enclosed cell where he will be held for a thousand years, awaiting his final judgment.

Verse 3. There's one mysterious sidebar in all this. For some reason known only to God and His all-wise, eternal plans, He's going to turn Satan loose for a "short time" after his thousand-year stint in the bad place. Apparently, from what we gather in verses 7-10, Satan is going to have one last gasp to deceive the believers . . . some form of final testing that is allowed under God's sovereign permission. Will some rebel against God, even this late in the game? We know Satan will somehow gather an end-time army numbering in the "sand of the sea" range (verse 8). This is a hard thing to grapple with, but it certainly shows that God is confident enough in His own victory to give Satan much more leeway than he deserves.

20:4-6 The Thousand-Year Reign

This is the moment when all those believers who had died before this time, including those who paid with their lives for refusing to cave to the antichrist's demands, will come back to life in a new resurrected body. They will all be part of the "first resurrection" (verse 6).

John doesn't tell us much more about what this period will be like, but apparently (this is speculation):

- Jesus' appearing will heal the earth's wounds from battle scars caused by years of judgment
- Resurrected believers will cohabit the earth with those who have not yet died
- Those who have not died will continue their normal lives of marrying, having children, living, and dying
- The resurrected will no longer marry (Matthew 22:30) or experience death again
- The ones who haven't been resurrected yet will still bear Adam's sin and be capable of unbelief

Even with no Satan around to bother them, these mere mortals will still be able to tempt themselves with evil, like we do (James 1:13-15). And because of what happens in verses 7-8, we know they'll still be susceptible to Satan's

ISRAEL'S RETURN.
The millennial reign of Christ will be the fulfillment of many great prophecies about Israel, such as Jeremiah's vision of a time when God will "place My law within them" (Jeremiah 31:34) and Ezekiel's prediction of their change of heart (Ezekiel 36:22-28).

PRIESTS OF GOD.
The New Testament teaches us that believers in Christ are part of a new covenant structure, which no longer requires people to need priests to speak to God for them. Instead, we are considered "a royal priesthood" ourselves (1 Peter 2:9), with access to the Father through our great high priest, Jesus Christ (Hebrews 4:14-16).

FIRST RESURRECTION.
Other Scriptures that shed light on this period in future history are 1 Corinthians 15:12-23, as well as the trumpet call of 1 Thessalonians 4:13-18.

deception when he turns up again.

"The rest of the dead," though—the deceased unbelievers—will have to wait this part out. Won't they be disappointed to learn, however, that when they come to life in a thousand years, it will only be for judgment and to be dispatched to their "second death" (see verses 13-14)—their final banishment to hell.

20:7-10 Satan's Last Stand . . . and Fall

BELOVED CITY.
It's hard to see this as anything other than Jerusalem, knowing how Jesus loved the city and its inhabitants (Luke 13:34). But it could just mean the place where God's people dwell, or perhaps God's people themselves.

In almost every good mystery movie, the scene that seems like the end isn't really the end. Just when things appear to have been settled, just when things have quieted down, just when you've taken a deep breath—WHAM!—in comes the unexpected surprise! The bad guy is back, fighting on sheer willpower, making one last stab at survival.

If you read this passage at face value, this surely seems to be what we're looking at here—Satan taking one more opportunity to deceive and defeat. But again, just like every time in the past, before he can even light the first fuse, BOOM!—God takes one good look at him and sees his doom.

So now the satanic trinity—Satan, the antichrist, and the false prophet—are back together again in their final resting place. Make that, restless place, for there "they will be tormented day and night forever and ever" (verse 10).

GOG AND MAGOG.
These mythical terms for the leader (Gog) of the land (Magog) that lead Satan's armies in opposition of Christ are unknown, as far as specifics go. We do know, however, that the same fate that befalls them in Ezekiel 38—39
—consuming fire from heaven
—gets them again in this show's-over passage from Revelation.

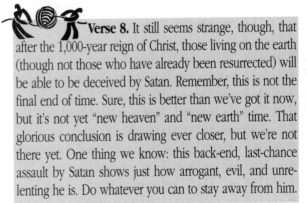

Verse 8. It still seems strange, though, that after the 1,000-year reign of Christ, those living on the earth (though not those who have already been resurrected) will be able to be deceived by Satan. Remember, this is not the final end of time. Sure, this is better than we've got it now, but it's not yet "new heaven" and "new earth" time. That glorious conclusion is drawing ever closer, but we're not there yet. One thing we know: this back-end, last-chance assault by Satan shows just how arrogant, evil, and unrelenting he is. Do whatever you can to stay away from him.

20:11-15 The Great White Throne

This is judgment day.

First, for the unbeliever:

If you've ever been called on the carpet for setting off a firecracker in the school bathroom, or cheating on a history test, or causing trouble in chemistry class, you know that anxious feeling of being caught, awaiting a verdict, and knowing you have to live with the consequences.

But you'd have to multiply that feeling a million times before you could feel the quivering knees of this final judgment appearance for the unsaved. If you do something stupid at school, you might get away with a slap on the wrist. At the "great white throne," however, the only outcome is the "lake of fire." No appeal. No grievance committee. No phone calls to your parents. No questions asked.

It's also judgment day for the believer:

Perhaps you *also* know what it's like to be accused of something you didn't do. You go to the principal's office, trying to defend yourself, but in the back of your mind you know there's always a chance you'll still take the rap for it. Not at the great white throne. Your position as a believer in Christ absolutely assures you that there is no chance of being misunderstood, of your name being thrown out on a technicality or a clerical error. You're in. You're staying in. And there's nothing the Devil can do about it.

Some people look at the judgment in this passage as being one single event, when the saved and the unsaved are sent either to heaven or hell. Others, however—premillennialists in particular—see at least two things going on here:

• *The judgment seat for believers.* This accounts for the "books" that are opened in the first part of verse 12. In this experience, believers (and perhaps unbelievers) are judged, not for salvation, but for the way they lived, the way they used the gifts and potential entrusted to them by God while on earth. They will all be rewarded accordingly . . . somehow.

ANNIHILATIONISM.
One idea you can discount by reading this passage is the notion that we all just turn into worm food and peat moss when we die. This depressing belief is what drives a lot of the hopeless, pointless mood in much of today's music, movies, and art. Another casualty at the judgment seat is the theory of reincarnation. We don't keep coming back to earth as other beings and things until we learn to get it right. "It is appointed for people to die once—and after this, judgment" (Hebrews 9:27).

JUDGMENT OF THE NATIONS.
Some people also read passages like Joel 3:1-3 to mean that nations will be judged for the way they treated Israel.

• *The great white throne.* This judgment happens when "another book" is opened in the last half of verse 12. This "book of life" contains, not a ledger of good deeds, but simply the individual names of those who are Christ's by calling, who have believed in Him through faith. Those whose names are "not found written in the book of life" (verse 15) are cast into hell.

What difference should it make to you today, knowing that you will be held accountable for your actions—even if you're a believer? Is fear of judgment a worthy motivator? Or not?

_____

_____

_____

_____

Revelation 21

We want to congratulate you. The past several chapters have included some hard reading, filled with falling rocks and hideous beasts and blood flowing up to the horse's bridles. We've gagged at the stench of sin and melted like wax at the sight of dragons and demons with frogs oozing out of their mouths.

But we've hopefully learned one of the great truths of Revelation: things may get bad before they get better, but the best is sure to come for those who hang in there to the end.

Now for the good part—the *really* good part! If you like happy endings, you're going to love the way your life in Christ ends up. What a great way for this book and the whole Bible to close—with two full chapters dedicated to some of the most exquisite promises and incredible scenery you can possibly imagine.

21:1-8 The New Creation

New Heaven, New Earth (verses 1-2)

What comes to mind when you think of the city? Oh, sure, there are some fun things to do downtown, like going to concerts, eating at fancy restaurants, and watching Fourth of July fireworks over the river. But you don't have to scratch too deeply below the surface to find a city's yucky underbelly. Crime. Corruption. Seamy nightlife and cigarette butts in the sewers.

So if we told you that you're going to spend eternity living in a big city, would that surprise you? Would it help if we told you that it'll have:

- *No sorrow*—nothing to make you the least bit blue, disappointed, or edgy?
- *No death*—no natural disasters, no funeral homes, no obituaries in the paper?
- *No pain*—no sore throats, no broken hearts, no rejection letters to your applications?

Instead of looking like a loser dressed for a bad date, it will look like "a bride adorned for her husband" (verse 2) —every hair in place, every feature perfected, every detail considered.

This is our "new Jerusalem . . . coming down out of heaven from God." Not coming down to our old earth, which is cursed by sin and ravaged by judgment, but to a "new earth" scrubbed clean and new, the way it must have looked when Adam and Eve first opened their eyes and looked around.

Neither is it coming down from the old heaven but from a "new heaven," recreated into something more beautiful, spectacular, and mind-blowing than ever!

"In the beginning God created the heavens and the earth" (Genesis 1:1). In the end, He'll create it again. Better than ever!

THE SEA.
To the ancient Hebrews, the sea was always ominous, the place where monsters lived. It held nothing but fear and risk and danger. But the sea and its hazards will no longer exist in the new creation —only the fresh, sparkling "living water" of God [verse 6]. This is a whole new, beautiful world we're talking about.

FUTURE CITY.
Tired and weary believers across the ages have always looked up from their hard, difficult lives, from working the ground and enduring persecution, "looking forward to the city . . . whose architect and builder is God" [Hebrews 11:10]. You get this same emotion when you read Hebrews 12:22 and 13:14.

REVELATION REPEATS.
This incredible closing scene is such a fitting end to this next-to-last vision, because it picks up so many elements John wrote about in the first part of the book: Jesus as the "Alpha and the Omega" (1:8); Jesus as the One who wants His Word to be written, obeyed, and remembered (1:11); Jesus fulfilling promises to the "victor" (3:12).

INHERITANCE.
The desirability of an inheritance or a heritage from God is a common biblical theme. You see it in Psalm 16:5-6, Psalm 119:111, and Proverbs 3:35, for example.

A New Way of Life (verses 3-4)

Best of all, God will be there with us—yes, right in the middle of town, and in every place His people find to locate. What could be better than living in a perfect place, in perfect security, in perfect bodies, with our incredibly perfect God?

Isn't God with us now on earth? Yes. Won't He definitely be with His people when Jesus reigns on the earth during the millennium? Of course. But He's never been with us in quite the same way He will be in our "new earth." Even during the thousand years, there will be some grief and sadness, some longing and disappointment. In this new place, however, we'll have Him right where we can see Him.

Over and Done—Well Done (verses 5-8)

This appears to be the closing moment of the third vision of Revelation, which started in 17:1. It's the heavenly wrap-up to nearly four chapters worth of hardship, conflict, and bloodshed.

- Everything is "new."
- Christ has proven beyond doubt that His word is "faithful and true."
- So now "it is done!" You can pull the hands off the clocks.
- The "living water" more than satisfies our every thirst.
- We victors have received our eternal inheritance.

For a long time on earth, unbelievers looked so cool on the outside. They sounded so appealing. But now it's clear what they were really like on the inside:

- Cowards—afraid to deal honestly with God
- Murderers—haters or ignorers of all things godly
- Sexually immoral—thinking sex was everything and every form of sex was okay
- Sorcerers, idolaters—seeking substitutes to feed their spiritual hunger
- Liars—living lies they were deceived into believing

> Are you liking the looks of this yet? This new heaven and new earth? Try to describe the way it strikes you.
>
> _____
>
> _____
>
> _____
>
> _____

21:9-27 The New Jerusalem

This passage begins the fourth and final vision of Revelation, a closing, breathtaking look at our future reward and our faithful Redeemer.

A Place to Bring His Bride To (verses 9-21)

"Let me introduce you to my wife."

"Have you ever met my husband?"

One of these days, more than likely, you'll feel that proud thumpity-thump in your chest as you show your new spouse around at a reunion, or on a visit to your church back home, or to the old friend you ran into at the mall one night.

But did you ever think about Jesus feeling that same kind of joy and honor when He introduces *us* to the crowd—His "bride, the wife of the Lamb"? (verse 9). Not only has He blessed us with His undeserved affection, but He's even built us a new home—a new city—with more bells and whistles than you can fit in one little Bible chapter.

We'll try, though.

• *The gates*—twelve in all, three on each side, each with the smooth translucence of a polished pearl (verse 21) and manned by its own duty angel (verse 12), though they never need to be closed, because it's always daytime and there's no danger of intruders (see verse 25).

• *The walls*—massively tall, sparkling like jasper (a green jewel), dazzlingly bright as crystal, climbing to the staggering height of nearly 1,400 miles—miles! (verse 17).

THE BOWL ANGEL.

It's kind of neat, really, to think that God would send one of the same angels John had last seen pouring a bowl of God's wrath on Satan and the sinners (15:6), who had been his tour guide to Babylon the Great (17:1), to show him now around the new Jerusalem. When someone capable of so much power shows you so much respect, you know you're in God's mercy zone.

TWELVE.

We mentioned way back in chapter 7 that twelve is a common biblical number: the twelve apostles, twelve tribes of Israel. All the twelves and multiples of twelve in this passage merely indicate that this city is built on perfect, precise, biblical proportions.

CITIES.
Ancient cities were small, crowded, dirty, and dark. Animal and human waste littered the streets. People locked their doors after dark and bolted the city gates. Lighting was primitive. Everything was unreliable. Imagine the contrast this city provided the first-century reader.

HEAVEN AND EARTH.
Ephesians 1:10 is a fascinating verse that says God will "bring everything together in the Messiah, both things in heaven and things on earth in Him." The division we experience now between these two realms will some day be put back together. Heaven and earth will be one, united whole, under the full and complete authority of Jesus.

• *The foundation*—not some drab concrete slab, but twelve, powerful pillars, each crafted with its own precious stone (verses 19-20), sparing no expense.

• *The street*—blazing with the appearance of pure gold, yet clear, transparent glass. (Try to picture that combination.) Plus, the whole city is as long and wide as it is tall—more spacious, spectacular, and stunning than anything you can imagine.

Some Kind of Town (verses 22-27)

We've talked about what this city will look like. Now let's think about what it will be like, how it'll actually feel to live there:

• *It won't have a church building.* We build churches here on our "old" earth because we need a place to meet with God, houses of worship to be set apart as sacred and holy. To live in "new Jerusalem," though, is to live in one, big, never-ending experience of fellowship with Jesus.

• *It won't need a sun.* Or moon. Or stars. Or any kind of light source. Who needs them when God's glory floods everything with perfect lighting at all-day levels of ideal? Imagine the freedom of living with no darkness, no shadows, nowhere to not know exactly what's going on.

• *It will have nations and kings.* We're all going to live in perfect unity and harmony, but not like plain vanilla, cookie-cutter, equal identities. We'll all have fulfilling work to do together, live in thriving governments, operate as individuals with our own personalities, interests, and gifts.

• *It will have no evil.* We won't even be able to tempt ourselves with jelly doughnuts. But that's not to say there won't be jelly doughnuts around. If it's good, it'll be there. Everything will be perfect, available to us with all its original properties and possibilities. Pure satisfaction.

Based on some of these imagination starters, what else do you think eternal life with Christ will be like? What are you hoping for? Is there any reason it couldn't be?

_____

_____

_____

PEOPLE VALUE.

One of the cool things you see in this chapter is the high value God places on mankind. We are indeed the crown of His creation. Even the angels, who appear so big and superior to us now, will be in subjection to us (1 Corinthians 6:3), amazed at this redemption God has given to us (1 Peter 1:12). This is one reason why right-to-life causes (abortion, euthanasia) are worth fighting for. Human life is supremely precious to its Creator.

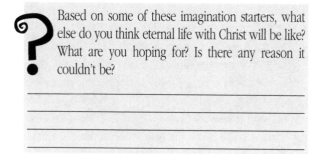

Revelation 22

22:1-5 The River of Life

Today's modern cities, especially the ones who place a high value on the environment and the quality of life for its citizens, work hard to build and maintain parks and greenways, sidewalks and bike trails, places where people have room to move, relax, and get comfortable.

That's nice.

People plant trees and flowers in their yards, private clubs and volunteers pick up trash along the roadside, and neighborhoods band together to make sure their communities are peaceful places where nature and beauty can flourish.

That's . . . nice.

But this desire for leaves, lawns, and landscapes is really a desire for God. It's the human hunger for:

WATER.
The Bible uses the analogy of water to describe the life-giving refreshment of God's Spirit. Jesus Himself referred to this when speaking to the woman at the well (of all places) in John 4:10-15.

TREE OF LIFE.
We mentioned this life-giving source when it showed up in chapter 2. It had a central place in the garden of Eden (Genesis 2:9), of course, but its appearance in heaven seems to be more like a whole bank of trees, each yielding its year-round fruit, fed by the water of God's Spirit, and no longer beyond the reach of His people.

SEALED PROPHECY.
When Daniel received his vision of history, he was told to "keep these words secret and seal the book until the time of the end" (Daniel 12:4). That time finally came for God to reveal to us His words to Daniel. The time is here, as well, for us to share the truths of Revelation.

- a "river of living water, sparkling like crystal"
- a "broad street" running through "the city" of God
- a "tree of life" that offers "healing" every day—"every month"—to the nations of the world

This world of ours can look mighty amazing and majestic in spots: the Grand Canyon, the Everglades, a summer sunset over a mid-western sky, the brilliance of autumn in the Northeast. But every time you see something beautiful in nature, remember that you're looking at a world that's groaning under a "curse" (verse 3). Imagine what it will be like to see God's glory on display in a new earth, where "night will no longer exist," where we will always "see His face," and where we'll never have to tear ourselves away, because we'll be reigning with Him there "forever and ever" (verse 5).

22:6-21 Epilogue

The Time Is Near (verses 6-13)

Have you ever experienced something so wonderful—like an unusually special Christmas, or the winning of a long sought-after award, or the recovery of a friend or family member from a serious injury—that you almost didn't know if you could stand any more joy and happiness? It felt so good, it was so incredibly sweet, you were just full to overflowing.

John must have found himself feeling that way, because in verse 8—after his virtual reality tour of heaven had piled blessing on top of blessing, promise on top of promise, hope on top of hope—he lost it. He fell down to worship "at the feet of the angel" who had shown him all these things.

It took a minute for him to pull himself together. It even took a pretty stern rebuke from the angel. But when John finally got his head fixed back into place, the angel reminded him what all this revelation was about.

Like George Bailey in *It's a Wonderful Life*, John had been given a special gift—the chance to see "what must quickly take place" (verse 6). His job now was not to sit on it, not to bask in its glory himself, but to tell his friends, to tell the church, to tell the world. He was not to "seal the prophetic words of this book" (verse 10) and keep its message quiet, because too much was at stake, and time was slipping by.

It still is.

Come On (verses 14-21)

Now we close this incredible book. It's really something, isn't it? We hope you've seen things that have encouraged you enough to stay the course, have given you a profound sense of God's awesomeness, sin's complete destructiveness, and God's amazing love for you.

Life—like the message of the Bible—all comes down to this: There are those who humble themselves and "wash their robes" in the cleansing, forgiving, purifying blood of Christ. And there are those who refuse to give up their love for pleasure, cheap excitement, selfish thrills, and dishonest pursuits. You can't have both. It has to be one or the other.

Listen to the ones who know the only right answer to this ultimate question of life or death:

- "The Spirit"—who knows everything, "even the deep things of God" (1 Corinthians 2:10).
- "The bride"—the redeemed who have already experienced a taste of their reward.
- And Jesus Himself—who loved you enough to die for you, and who loves you enough to warn you of His soon return (verse 20).

They're all calling you to come to the "living water" and receive it as the gift for your thirsty soul (verse 17). They're calling you to love and deal reverently with the Word of God as it's presented in the Scriptures (verses 18-19). They're calling you to experience the "grace of the Lord Jesus" that can purify your heart and give you a fresh start, a real hope, and even a new reputation, if you need one (verse 21).

They're calling you home.

WORSHIPING ANGELS.
Idolizing angels was one of the spiritual sidelines that people had already gotten off track with in New Testament times (Colossians 2:18). Sure, angels are mind-boggling enough to amaze you, and it's fine to be interested in how they work, but be careful that you don't fall for putting them on too high of a pedestal.

? You coming?

If you liked "NEVER SAY DIE"
[Getting Deep in the Book of Revelation] . . .
Check out these other TruthQuest Commentaries:

UP CLOSE WITH JESUS
Getting Deep in the Book of Luke
ISBN 0-8054-2852-6

A LIFE AND DEATH EXPERIENCE
Getting Deep in the Book of Romans
ISBN 0-8054-2857-7

CHRISTIAN TO THE CORE
Getting Deep in the Book of James
ISBN 0-8054-2853-4